The TROUBLE With
Longtails

The TROUBLE With Longtails

Mary H. Duplex

Pacific Press Publishing Association
Boise, Idaho
Montemorelos, Nuevo Leon, Mexico
Oshawa, Ontario, Canada

Designed by Tim Larson
Cover Art by Francis Livingston
Edited by Lincoln Steed

Copyright © 1986 by
Pacific Press Publishing Association
Printed in United States of America
All Rights Reserved

Library of Congress Cataloging in Publication Data

Duplex, Mary H.
　The trouble with longtails.

　Summary: Third-grader Trish discovers that pet rats can be fun,
trouble, and a way of gaining confidence and making new friends.
　1. Rats as pets—Juvenile literature. [1. Rats as pets] I. Title
SF459.R3D86　　1986　　　626'.93233　　　85-25866
ISBN 0-8163-0627-3

86 87 88 89 • 4 3 2 1

Dedicated to—
Linda, Patty, Renae, Jeff, and Peg—who first introduced me to
Longtails.

Contents

1. Trish to the Rescue 9
2. Rats Before Breakfast 15
3. Almost Best Friends 21
4. A Surprise for Trish 27
5. Sally the Brave 33
6. It's a Secret 39
7. More Room 47
8. Narrow Escape 55
9. The Big Day 63
10. Trouble With Longtails 69
11. Mr. Plunkett Helps 73
12. No Place for Rats 79
13. Trish Speaks Up 87
14. Rats and Roller Skates 91

Trish to the Rescue

Clutching the big brown paper sack in her arms, Trish Delaney hurried down Thackery Street. She peeked into the sack, through the wire top of the cage, and smiled. "You don't have to be afraid anymore," she said. "You're safe now."

A gust of cold wind swirled fallen leaves across the sidewalk. Trish walked faster. Turning in at the apartment building where she lived, Trish rushed up the steps. She balanced the sack on one knee and folded the top of the sack over.

"I'll take you out as soon as I get home," she whispered. "Don't make any noise. Mrs. Peabody might hear you."

Cautiously, Trish opened the door and peeked inside. The hall was empty. Trish tiptoed across to the elevator and pushed the button. The down arrow came on. Trish looked up and down the hall while she waited. There was no one in sight.

The elevator door slid open at last—and there stood old Mrs. Peabody. Trish hugged the sack closer and wished Mrs. Peabody hadn't picked this time to come down. Mrs. Peabody's thin mouth pulled down at the corners when she saw Trish. Her bushy eyebrows came together in a disapproving frown.

"What have you been up to?" Mrs. Peabody demanded.

Trish tried to answer, but her tongue stuck to the roof of her mouth the way it always did when she met the old lady unexpectedly in the hall. It was almost as bad as when Mrs. Martin called on her to recite in class. Only her teacher was much nicer than Mrs. Peabody.

Mrs. Peabody thumped her cane on the floor. "Speak up!" she

snapped. "What's the matter, cat got your tongue?"

The sack wiggled a little. Trish wished Mrs. Peabody hadn't mentioned cats. She gulped. "I'm on my way home from school." Trish got the words out in a rush.

"Humph!" Mrs. Peabody snorted. "Your sister Lynne came home twenty minutes ago."

Trish edged past the old woman. "I have to go now," she said politely. She stepped quickly into the elevator and pushed the button for the fourth floor. Mrs. Peabody stumped off down the hall toward the manager's office.

The elevator door closed. Trish sagged against the back wall with a sigh of relief. Mrs. Peabody lived on the fourth floor too, in the end apartment. She spent all her time snooping around the halls. She reported every little thing to Mr. Wilson, the manager. Trish was glad she hadn't asked what was in the sack.

Trish got off on the fourth floor and stopped at her own door. Now that she was in the third grade she had a key of her own. She wore it on a chain around her neck. But she was afraid to put down the sack. Mrs. Peabody might come back up in the elevator before she got the door open. Trish rang the doorbell.

Lynne opened the door. Glancing at the sack, she asked, "What did you bring home this time?"

Trish ignored her question and went into the living room. She put the sack down gently on the coffee table and brushed the wind-whipped strands of red hair back from her face.

Mother looked up from the sweater she was knitting for Lynne and frowned. "Trish, where have you been? You know you're supposed to come straight home from school."

"I'm not very late." Trish struggled out of her coat and laid it over the arm of the sofa. "I just stopped to watch the moving men load a big van down the street."

Fredrick wandered in from the kitchen. His blue eyes lit up when he saw the sack. "Did you bring me something?" he said. "Let me see!"

Trish put her arm around the sack. Sometimes Mrs. Martin gave her extra papers to bring home. She always gave some to Fredrick so he could play school. "Not this time," she said. "This is mine." Fredrick's lip began to quiver.

"You can see it in a minute," Trish said.

Lynne sat down and swung her long legs over the arm of the chair. She twirled a strand of her dark hair around a finger. "I bet it's more junk," she said.

Trish pulled the sack closer. "It is not! Just because you're eleven you think you know everything."

Mother laid her knitting in her lap. "It must be something important, Trish. Show us what it is."

"Just wait until you hear what happened," Trish said as she tore open the sack. "This awful boy—"

Mother gasped. Trish looked up. She hadn't seen Mother move, but suddenly Mother was standing behind her chair.

"Are those rats?" Mother's voice sounded funny.

Trish grinned with pride. "Aren't they cute? That's Mrs. Longtails," she said, pointing to a brown-and-white rat. "And the black one is Mr. Longtails." Fredrick moved closer to the cage. "I came along just in time," Trish said. "The mean boy that owned them was going to take them to the zoo and feed them to the snakes!" Trish shivered.

"Ha!" Lynne sneered. She got up and peered through the glass side of the cage. "These rats belonged to Rory Johnson. He's been trying to give them to everybody in the fifth grade for the last week. He even tried to give them to me." Mrs. Longtails sat up. She stretched her neck toward Lynne and wiggled her whiskers. "Ugh!" Lynne backed away and sat down again. "Rory Johnson wasn't really going to feed them to the snakes. He just said that so you would take them."

"How do you know?" Trish asked suspiciously.

"Lynne is right," Mother said. "No one is allowed to feed the snakes at the zoo except the keepers."

"Oh," Trish said in a small voice. "I never thought of that."

"Now," Mother said, staying a safe distance from the cage, "you take those rats right back to this Rory Johnson and tell him you can't keep them."

Trish put her hands behind her back and dug her toe into the carpet. "I can't," she said at last. "Rory moved away. The moving van took all of the Johnson's things."

Lynne nodded in agreement. "That's right, Mom. That's why

Rory has been trying to give the rats away. His mother promised him a dog if he got rid of them before they moved."

Mother glanced at the rats and sighed. "I can see why," she said.

Fredrick poked his finger through the wire-mesh top and wiggled it. Mr. Longtails's nose began to twitch. He crept across the top of the little wooden box in the cage and sat up. He sniffed, then stood on his hind legs. He took Fredrick's finger in his tiny paws and sniffed again.

"Look out!" Mother shrieked. "He might bite!"

Fredrick jerked his hand back and laughed. "You scared me!" he said.

"They won't bite," Trish said. She started to lift the top of the cage. "Rory let me hold Mrs. Longtails. They're tame. Honest."

Mother took a step backward and pointed her finger at Trish. "Don't you dare open that cage in here. I won't have those things running loose."

Trish pushed the top of the cage back in place. "Is it all right if I open it in my room?" she asked.

Lynne leaped from her chair. "You're not going to take those awful things in my room!" she declared.

"It's my room too," Trish reminded her.

"Mother!" Lynne howled. "You're not going to let her keep them, are you?"

"You have a whole shelf of horses, and Fredrick has his tigers," Trish said. "I guess I can have pets if I want them."

"Trish," Mother said, "you know very well that Lynne's horses are made of china and Fredrick's tigers are only toys. This is not the same thing at all."

"And besides," Lynne announced triumphantly, "pets are not allowed."

"Goldfish are allowed," Trish argued. "And the rats are just like goldfish, except they don't swim in water."

"They are not!" Lynne shot back.

Mother looked from Lynne to Trish and back again. "We will settle this when your father comes home. Until then, Trish, you may take them in your room." Trish grinned and picked up the cage.

Lynne crossed her arms and glared at Trish. "Bet Dad won't let you keep them," she said.

"Bet he will."

"Mr. Wilson won't," Lynne said with a smug look on her face.

"Pets are allowed if they're in cages," Trish said. She started down the hall to her room. Fredrick tagged along behind her.

Trish pushed the door shut with her foot. She put the cage down on her shelf beside the window and sat down on the floor to watch the rats. Fredrick knelt beside her. The rats sat very still for a minute and looked around. Then Mrs. Longtails scampered over to the feed dish and began to eat. She picked up the seeds in her tiny paws and nibbled hungrily.

"Can I hold one?" Fredrick asked. "Please, Trish. I'll be real careful. I promise."

Trish got up and went to make sure the door was closed tight. It would never do for the rats to get out. Mom would really be angry. Trish glanced around the room. The closet door was open, but the rats couldn't get out. She sat down beside Fredrick and opened the cage.

"I'll let you hold Mr. Longtails if you promise not to squeeze him."

Fredrick nodded eagerly. "I promise! I'll hold him real easy. I won't squeeze him a bit."

Trish hesitated. Fredrick was only four. He had never held a live animal before. "If he scares you, don't hurt him," she warned again. "He might bite you." Trish picked up the rat and held him out. "Pet him first so he won't be afraid of you." Fredrick ran his hand gently down Mr. Longtails's back. "Now hold out your arm." Trish put Mr. Longtails on Fredrick's wrist. Mr. Longtails sat up, then scampered up Fredrick's sleeve to his shoulder. Fredrick squeezed his eyes half shut and giggled under his breath.

The rat sniffed Fredrick's ear. "That tickles," Frederick whispered, trying his best to hold still. "I think he likes me."

Mrs. Longtails had finished eating, so Trish reached into the cage and picked her up. She put Mrs. Longtails on her shoulder. The rat's whiskers brushed against Trish's neck and she jumped. It felt funny and tickled at the same time. It was going to be fun having live pets. Mrs. Longtails ran down the front of Trish's shirt and onto the floor.

Mrs. Longtails's whiskers twitched busily as she explored the room. She ran along the baseboard and into the closet. Trish watched to see what she would do.

Fredrick giggled suddenly. "She jumped in your roller skates, Trish!"

"That's not mine; it's Lynne's. I don't like roller skates." Trish got up to rescue the rat.

"I like roller skates," said Fredrick. "When I get big I'm going to learn to skate."

"You won't think it's so much fun when you skin your knees and almost break your arm like I did the first time I tried it," Trish said. "I'm never going to roller-skate again."

They heard the front door close. "Daddy's home!" Fredrick shouted. He leaped to his feet and started for the door.

Trish grabbed him by the back of the shirt. "Quick, give me Mr. Longtails. I have to put him back in the cage."

"I want to show him to Daddy," Fredrick protested.

"Mom won't let me keep them if you take him out there," Trish warned.

Fredrick handed her the rat and jerked open the door. "Daddy, come see what Trish's got!" he shouted as he ran down the hall.

Trish heard Lynne's voice as she put the rats back in the cage. "Oh no! I wanted to talk to Dad first." Trish's insides felt all squeezed together. "What if Dad doesn't like my new pets either?"

Rats Before Breakfast

Dad grinned at Trish as Fredrick pulled him into the room. "Well, what's all this I hear about your owning livestock?" he teased.

Trish clasped her hands behind her back and giggled. "Oh, Dad, it's only two rats!"

Dad squatted on his heels and looked into the cage. "So this is what all the fuss is about," he said.

Fredrick leaned against Dad's shoulder and watched the rats. "They're neat," he said. "They can climb up your arm and tickle you. Trish let me hold one."

"Please may I keep them?" Trish begged.

Dad rubbed his jaw thoughtfully. "I'm afraid there are rules about keeping pets here, Trish."

"Goldfish are allowed," Trish said. "You can ask Mr. Wilson and tell him I'll keep them in their cage. If he says it's all right, can I keep them? Please, Dad. They won't be any trouble. And I'll buy their food with my allowance."

"Let me think about it." Dad stood up. "Run along, both of you, and wash up for dinner."

Trish helped Fredrick wash his face and hands. "Hurry up," she said as he paddled his hands in the water. "Let's go see if Dad will let me keep the rats." Fredrick dried his hands quickly, and they hurried into the dining room.

Mom and Dad and Lynne were already at the table. Trish slid into her chair and waited until Dad asked the blessing before she looked at him hopefully. Before she could say anything, Dad smiled.

"I called Mr. Wilson," he said. "He has no objections to the rats as long as they are caged. I see no reason why you shouldn't keep them."

Trish let her breath out in a whoosh. "Oh, Dad! Thank you!" she cried.

"Oh gross!" Lynne moaned. "I'll never be able to sleep with those awful things in my room."

Dad chuckled. "I think you'll survive, Lynne." He finished filling Fredrick's plate and passed it to Mom. "You might even get to like the rats."

"Ugh! Not me!" Lynne shivered.

"I do!" Fredrick shouted happily.

Mom stopped cutting up Fredrick's dinner and looked at Dad. "Really, Mark, do you think this is a wise decision?"

"It's time Trish learned responsibility," Dad answered. "She's old enough, and the rats are too small to create a problem."

"Does it have to be rats?" Mother asked.

Dad grinned. "Rats are better than a canary. At least they won't wake you up at five o'clock in the morning."

"Well, I suppose we can let you keep them on a trial basis, Trish," Mother agreed. "See that you keep them in your room. I don't want them out here."

"I will," Trish promised. She was almost too excited to eat. When dinner was over she raced for her room.

"You have to help with the dishes," Lynne called after her.

"I'm going to feed my pets first," Trish answered. Lynne doesn't know how wonderful it is to have live pets of your very own, she thought.

Lynne usually spent a lot of time in their room, but tonight she waited until bedtime to come in. "Are those things in their cage?" she asked from the doorway. "I'm not going to sleep in here if they're out running around."

"They're in the cage," Trish assured her. "Come see for yourself."

"I don't want them near my bed," Lynne said as she inched her way into the room. She looked over at the cage.

"Why don't you hold one; then you won't be afraid of them

anymore." Trish started to hop out of bed.

"I don't want to hold one." Lynne struggled into her night-gown and said her prayers before she got into bed. "I don't want to look at them either." Lynne turned her back and pulled the covers up over her ear.

Trish switched off the lamp between their beds. "Good night," she said. Lynne didn't answer. Trish lay very still and listened to the soft rustling sounds coming from the cage as she drifted off to sleep.

Trish woke earlier than usual the next morning. She raised up on one elbow and looked at the rats to make sure it hadn't been a dream. Mr. Longtails popped his head up out of the cedar shavings on the bottom of the cage and disappeared again. The shavings raised up in a ridge as he tunneled through them. Mrs. Longtails was sitting on top of the little wooden box wash-ing her face. Trish glanced over at Lynne. She was lying on her back with her arms above her head, still fast asleep. Trish slipped out of bed and took the top off the cage.

"Hi," Trish whispered to Mrs. Longtails. She held out her hand. Mrs. Longtails wiggled her whiskers and scampered up Trish's arm. Trish giggled silently as Mrs. Longtails burrowed under the collar of her pajamas. Mr. Longtails stopped making tunnels and came to see what Trish was doing.

"Do you want to get picked up too?" Trish whispered. She scooped him up and settled herself cross-legged in the middle of her bed. She put Mr. Longtails on her shoulder.

Mrs. Longtails crept out from under Trish's collar and crawled down the front of her pajamas to her pocket. Trish watched as Mrs. Longtails sniffed around inside, half in and half out of her pocket.

Suddenly Mr. Longtails leaped from her shoulder and landed in the middle of Lynne's stomach.

Lynne's eyes flew open. She took one look at the rat and screamed. Mr. Longtails disappeared in the folds of the blan-ket. Lynne sat straight up and screamed again. Trish grabbed Mrs. Longtails and jumped off the bed. She searched frantically among Lynne's covers. Lynne saw Mrs. Longtails in Trish's hand and screamed again.

"Be quiet. You're scaring the rats," Trish told her.

The door flew open. "What's going on in here?" Dad demanded. His hair was standing up in little tufts, and he only had one slipper on.

"What's happened?" Mother asked breathlessly, still trying to find the other half of the belt to her robe.

"That rat attacked me!" Lynne shrieked.

"He did not!" Trish ran her hand down a fold in the blanket. "Sit still. You're going to squash Mr. Longtails."

Lynne gasped and pulled her knees up under her chin. "Get him away from me!"

"I'm trying to," Trish told her.

"What's the matter?" Fredrick asked, still rubbing sleep from his eyes. "You woke me up."

The doorbell rang one long continuous buzz. Mother rushed to answer it. Just then Mr. Longtails scurried out of the blanket near Lynne's hand. Trish rescued him as Lynne bolted from the bed and hid behind Dad.

"He was going to bite me!" Lynne cried.

"He was not. Stop being such a sissy," Trish said disgustedly. "You wouldn't hurt her, would you?" She stroked Mr. Longtails gently.

"He would too! I saw his teeth!" Lynne insisted.

"That will do!" Dad shouted. He really sounded cross. "Trish, put those rats back in their cage, and be quick about it." Trish rushed to obey.

"And keep them there." Mother's face looked tight and angry as she came back into the room. "That was Mrs. Peabody at the door wanting to know what all the screaming was about. She's probably on her way down to tell Mr. Wilson all about it right this minute. Trish, I don't want those rats out of the cage again."

"But, Mom," Trish protested.

"You heard what your mother said. Do it, and no arguments," Dad said. He was really in a bad mood. Trish put the rats in the cage and closed the top.

"Now that we're all awake, I may as well fix breakfast," Mother said. She left the room and started down the hall.

"I want cereal," Fredrick shouted and trotted after her.

"I get the bathroom first," Lynne announced. She snatched up her robe and stalked out of the room.

Trish sat down on the edge of her bed. "What's the use of having pets if I can't play with them?" she asked.

Dad stuck his hand in the pocket of his robe and leaned against the door frame. "You'll have to admit being awakened by a rat is not very pleasant, even if you like them," he said.

Trish looked down at her hands and nodded. "I didn't mean to scare Lynne. I only wanted to play with the rats. I didn't know Mr. Longtails could jump that far."

"I'm sure you didn't," Dad agreed. "I think you should learn more about their habits before you take them out of the cage again. It's not like having a dog or cat, you know."

"I will," Trish said. "And I'll tell Lynne I'm sorry."

"A very good idea," Dad said. "We'll talk more about it later. Now get ready for breakfast." He yawned and went back to his room.

Everyone had calmed down by the time breakfast was over and Trish was ready for school.

"Trish," Mother said. "I think it's time to make a few rules. You may take the rats out of the cage when Lynne is not in the room. Remember, it's Lynne's room too. So you can't spend all of your time in there playing with the rats."

Trish threw her arms around Mother's neck. "I will. I'll do everything you said. You won't even know the rats are here."

Lynne sneezed. "I will," she said under her breath.

Almost Best Friends

Trish ran all the way to the school crossing. Since Melody moved away the previous summer there had been no girls in her class living on Thackery Street. Then last weekend Sally Santini's family moved into an apartment down the block. Trish had walked partway home with Sally yesterday. She hoped now they would walk to school together every day. She could hardly wait to tell Sally about the rats.

There were several boys and girls waiting at the crossing. But there was no sign of Sally. Trish waited while Mr. Bailey, the street patrol, stopped traffic and let the children cross.

"Morning, Trish," Mr. Bailey called. "You waiting for somebody?"

"I'm waiting for Sally," Trish answered. Mr. Bailey had been on this same corner since long before Trish started kindergarten. He knew all of the children that crossed here. Even if they were new in the neighborhood.

Mr. Bailey put one hand on his hip. He lifted his cap and scratched his gray head with the other. "Let me see now," he said thoughtfully. "Sally? That would be the new girl with long, dark hair and roller skates."

"That's right," Trish said eagerly. "Has she come yet?"

Mr. Bailey nodded. "Yep. She was one of the first ones to cross this morning. Said she wanted to do some roller-skating before school started."

Trish tried to hide her disappointment. "Thanks, Mr. Bailey. I better cross now," she said.

Mr. Bailey signaled the cars to stop. "Don't you go poking along now," he warned. "Or you'll be late."

Trish smiled and waved. Mr. Bailey said that to everybody. "See you after school," she called.

Trish scuffed through the fallen leaves as she walked along. Sally had talked about roller-skating yesterday. She didn't seem to be interested in anything else. Trish stopped to catch a big yellow maple leaf floating down from the tree above her. Skating wasn't any fun. If only Sally liked to do something else, they could have lots of fun together. Suddenly Trish stopped. I know! she thought. I'll ask Sally to come home with me after school to see the rats. Maybe she will like them so much she will forget all about roller-skating. Trish tossed the leaf in the air and ran the rest of the way to school.

Someone tugged hard on the back of Trish's coat as she hurried down the hall to Mrs. Martin's room. Trish turned around.

"What are you looking at?" Herbie Fletcher asked. He crossed his eyes and stretched his face out of shape until all of the freckles on his cheeks seemed to run together.

"You're a pest!" Trish said. She hoped he would go away. Instead, he followed her into the room.

Stanley and Joe were the only ones there. Herbie went back to the science table to see what they were doing. Trish put her things away and hurried back outside.

She found Sally skating alone near the monkey bars. "Hi!" Trish called. Sally waved and skated toward her. "I wanted to walk with you today," Trish said, "but you had already gone."

Sally skated in a circle around her. "Angelia and Cindy were supposed to bring their skates and roller-skate with me this morning. But they forgot. I wish you had a pair of skates. We could skate together after school."

"I have some new pets," Trish said, hoping to change the subject.

Sally leaned on her right toe stop. "I've got a cat named Muffin. What have you got?"

"Two rats," Trish said proudly.

"Oh." Sally skated over to the steps and sat down to take off her skates.

Trish said down beside her. "Would you like to come over and see them after school? They're really cute."

Sally bent over to unfasten her skate strap. "I can't. I have to go to the dentist right after school. My mom is picking me up." She didn't sound even a little bit interested in the rats.

"I'm going to ask Mrs. Martin if I can bring them to school," Trish said. "Nobody ever brought rats to our room before." She tried to make it sound very important.

Sally unfastened her other strap without looking up. "What's so special about that?"

"Well, first you have to ask Mrs. Martin's permission to bring them. She doesn't let just any pet come to school. And second," Trish counted off on her fingers, "you have to have all of your work done. You know, not be behind in your workbooks or anything. Then you have to get up in front of—the whole—class." Her voice trailed off.

Why didn't I remember that part before I told Sally about bringing the rats? Trish thought miserably. I can't get up in front of the whole class. I would never remember what I'm supposed to say. Now what am I going to do?

"Get up in front of the whole class and what?" Sally asked.

"You have to tell all about your pets," Trish said gloomily. "Where they come from, whether it's another country, and whether they are helpful to man in some way. Stuff like that."

Sally dropped her skates on the step beside her and looked at Trish for the first time. "Do you know all those things about rats?"

"Not yet," Trish admitted. "But I have to learn. I took the rats out of the cage this morning, and one of them jumped right in the middle of my sister's stomach while she was still asleep."

Sally giggled. "I bet your sister was surprised."

Trish grinned. "It sounds funny now. But my mom and dad were really mad. Dad says I can't take the rats out of the cage again until I learn more about their habits." She leaned close to Sally. "Do you want to bring the rats to school with me? We could keep it a secret," she whispered.

"That's a neat idea," Sally said, catching some of Trish's enthusiasm. "Won't everybody be surprised?" She covered her mouth with her hand to smother her giggles. "We can learn about the rats. Then we can both stand up in front of the class and tell about them."

Trish couldn't believe her ears. Sally really *wanted* to stand up in front of the whole class. And she wanted to learn about the rats together. Why they were almost best friends already!

Suddenly Herbie charged down the steps and leaped in front of them. "I know a secret," he chanted.

Trish gasped. Herbie must have heard every word. Now he was going to spoil everything. He always did.

Sally grabbed up her skates. "Ignore him," she whispered. The girls jumped up and hurried away.

"Herbie is always teasing me," Trish said. "I wish he would go pick on somebody else."

Herbie ran around in front of them again. "I know a secret," he sang.

"You don't know anything," Sally said. "Go away and stop bothering us."

"That's what you think," Herbie jeered. "I know—" The bell rang. They all hurried into the classroom.

For the rest of the morning Trish wondered whether Herbie would tell her secret. Every time she looked back at him, Herbie crossed his eyes and made a face at her. She just knew he was going to tell and spoil everything.

A few minutes before lunch Mrs. Martin made an announcement. "For our next science project we will be studying about reptiles and their place in our environment. We will have film-strips on the larger reptiles in their natural habitat. However, I think you will all enjoy having some live reptiles right here in our classroom."

Scott raised his hand. "What kind of reptiles?" he asked.

Mrs. Martin smiled. "Snakes and lizards," she said. Herbie and the other boys voiced their approval.

"Oh ick!" Barbara mumbled.

Mrs. Martin laughed. "They will be confined in glass cases, and no one will be allowed to handle them." The class was still talking about the new project when the lunch bell rang.

When the class returned from lunch there were two large fish tanks on the science table in the back of the room. Everyone crowded around. The first tank had sand and cactus in the bottom. The second tank had plants and small stones. Trish saw the two small garter snakes coiled daintily among the plants in the second tank. But it took her a long time to find the two fat horned toads in the sand.

Herbie grinned at Trish and crossed his eyes when she started back to her seat. "Told you I knew a secret," he taunted.

Trish caught her breath. So that was it! Herbie had found out about the reptiles this morning from Stanley and Joe. He didn't know about the rats after all!

A Surprise for Trish

Trish and Sally stayed after school to ask Mrs. Martin about bringing the rats.

"They sound very interesting," Mrs. Martin said. "But I'm afraid you will have to wait until after our science project is over. Pets are not allowed when we have anything live in the classroom."

"Oh," Trish said. The girls started to turn away.

"Wait," Mrs. Martin said. She took out her schedule book and opened it. "Our project will be over in a couple of weeks. Let me see—" She ran her finger down the page. "Yes, here we are. You may bring the rats on October 15. Will that be all right?" Trish and Sally nodded. Mrs. Martin drew a red circle around the date in her book and wrote a note about the rats in the margin of the page. "Now don't forget."

"Thank you, Mrs. Martin," Trish and Sally said at the same time. They grinned at each other as they started for the door.

"Just a minute," Trish said. "I want to ask Mrs. Martin something." She hurried back to the teacher's desk. "Could we keep it a secret? About the rats, I mean. We want it to be a surprise."

Mrs. Martin smiled. "Of course," she said. "It will be a nice surprise for the whole class."

"Especially for the boys," Sally whispered as they hurried outside. The girls giggled. "Can't you just see Herbie's face when he sees the rats?" Sally said, as they ran down the school steps.

"I'm glad Mrs. Martin is going to let us bring the rats," Trish said. "It's going to be fun learning about them together."

"Oh, there's my mom," Sally said. "I forgot she was coming to pick me up. I wish I didn't have to go to the dentist. See you tomorrow."

"Meet me at Mr. Bailey's crossing," Trish called.

"Come early," Sally answered. She climbed into the car and waved at Trish as her mother drove away.

Trish hurried home to see the rats.

When Trish settled down in front of the cage to watch the rats, she noticed that their feed dish was almost empty. Trish wished she had thought to ask Rory Johnson what kind of food to feed them and where to buy it. She opened her top dresser drawer and took out some of the money she had been saving. Then she went to find her mother.

"I need some more food for my rats," Trish said when she found her mother in the kitchen. "I have my own money, but where should I go to buy food for them?"

Mother dusted the rolling pin with flour and sprinkled some on the dough on the cutting board. "There is a pet shop six blocks away, over on Connor Street."

"May Lynne come with me? I don't want to go that far by myself." Trish picked up a scrap of dough and rolled it between her fingers.

Mother rolled her mound of dough into a circle with quick, neat strokes. "Lynne is over at Deb's," she said. Maybe there is no need for you to go all the way to the pet shop. The Woolworth store around the corner carries pet supplies. Perhaps you can buy what you need there."

"I never thought of that." Trish dropped the little ball of dough back on the cutting board. "Is it all right if I go? I'll be right back."

Mother nodded. "But don't be gone too long. Dinner is almost ready. And be quiet going out. If Fredrick hears you, he'll want to go too."

Trish got her coat and hurried past the living room, where Fredrick was sprawled on the rug in front of the television.

When Trish reached the Woolworth store she walked all

around the pet section. It was just like a little pet shop. There were birds in cages, tanks of goldfish, and cages of hamsters. Trish stopped to look at them. The hamsters were curled up in little balls, fast asleep. Trish wondered what they did when they were awake. She went on to the shelves of pet food.

There were all kinds of boxes and cans, but none of them were marked Rat Food. Maybe the sales clerk knows what rats eat, Trish thought. She looked around. There were no clerks in sight. Trish turned down the aisle. She found a clerk stacking boxes on the shelf. Trish stopped and waited for her to finish.

"Hi," the clerk said. "What can I help you with today?" She was young and pretty and had a nice smile. The name tag on her green smock said Nancy Forrest.

"I need some food for my rats," Trish answered. "Do you know what they eat? The boy that gave them to me didn't tell me what to feed them."

Miss Forrest put down the box she was holding and walked back to the pet foods with Trish. She reached up on the shelf and brought down two boxes marked Rodent Mix.

"This is what you need," Miss Forrest said. "We have two brands. Which one would you like?"

Trish shrugged. "I'm not sure. Which would you choose?"

Miss Forrest held out the red-and-yellow box with a picture of a rat and a hamster on the front. "My aunt feeds this kind to her rats. It has almost everything they need. You should give them some fresh fruit and vegetables too," she added.

"I'll buy that one then," Trish said, reaching for the box. "Thank you for helping me."

"Miss Forrest smiled. "Good luck with your rats," she said and went back to where she had been working.

As Trish left the pet section she found a rack of books about pets at the end of the aisle. She stopped to look through them. There were books on the care and feeding of goldfish, hamsters, gerbils, turtles, birds, cats, dogs, and monkeys. I wish they had one on rats, Trish thought as she sorted through the books with their bright-colored covers. Behind a book on training poodles she found just what she had been looking for. She looked at the price of the book and counted her money. She had just enough to buy the rat food and the book too. Trish paid for them and hurried home.

Mrs. Peabody peeked out of her door as Trish got out of the elevator and started down the hall. Trish wondered whether the old lady sat behind her door and listened for the elevator to open. She pretended she didn't know Mrs. Peabody was watching her as she got out her key and turned it in the lock.

". . . and Julie said—Wait a minute, Deb." Lynne frowned as Trish closed the door. She turned her back and waited until Trish went on down the hall before she started talking again.

Trish wondered what Lynne and Deb spent so much time talking about. She passed the living room. Fredrick was still sprawled in front of the television with his chin in his hands. Trish went into her room and closed the door. "This time I get to have the rats all to myself." She opened the box of rodent mix and started to fill the feed dish.

Mr. Longtails stretched his neck out toward the dish and wiggled his nose. "I hope you and Mrs. Longtails like this kind," Trish said. He came over and started to eat. Trish giggled. "I guess you like it all right." Suddenly Trish noticed that Mrs. Longtails was missing. "Now how did she get out?" Quickly Trish searched the room. "Lynne will have a fit if I don't find her." She looked under the beds and in the closet. Trish covered the whole room before she gave up and went back to the cage.

Mr. Longtails scampered over to the side of the cage. He sat up and wiggled his whiskers. Trish bent down and examined the lid of the cage. It looked all right. "Where is Mrs. Longtails?" she asked the rat. "Did she get out of the cage and run away, or did Fredrick take her?" Trish straightened up. "I bet that's what happened. Oh, if he let her loose in the apartment Mom will really be mad." She started to turn toward the door, when Mrs. Longtails came out of the little wooden box. "There you are!" Trish cried. "I thought you were lost. What were you doing in there?"

Mrs. Longtails stared at Trish with her beady, black eyes, then scampered over to the feed dish and began to eat. Trish bent over and tried to peek into the little hole in the front of the box. It was too dark inside to see. I wonder if they have a nest in there? Trish thought. Lynne is always telling me my half of the room looks like a rat's nest, but I bet it doesn't look like that at all. She opened the cage and reached for the box. The top came off. Trish peeked inside and gasped. "Ohhh, what a wonderful surprise!" she whispered.

There, cuddled together in a heap, like a big wad of used bubblegum, was a nest of tiny, pink baby rats. They were smaller than Trish's little finger. Their eyes were closed, and they had no hair at all. Trish tried to count them. It was no use. Mrs. Longtails had dug a hole in the shavings she'd used to make the nest. The tiny rats were all piled together in it. Trish wondered how they could breathe that way. Quietly she put the lid back on the box.

"I wonder what Mom and Lynne are going to say when they find out about the babies." Mrs. Longtails stopped chewing and looked at Trish. "Don't worry. I'm not going to tell them until they get used to you," Trish said.

She took the water bottle off the side of the cage. "We will keep it a secret. Just the three of us." She went to the bathroom for fresh water. When she returned, Mrs. Longtails was gone again. Trish attached the water bottle to the side of the cage again. She checked the tube on the end of the bottle to make sure the water would come out when the rats wanted a drink. Then she put the mesh top back on the cage and picked up her new rat book.

"I'm glad the snakes and lizards came to school today." She flopped down on her bed, leaned on her elbows, and riffled through the pages of the book. "There is a lot to learn about rats in here." She glanced toward the cage and grinned. "And now I have a lot more rats to learn about."

Trish was still reading when Lynne came into the room. "Did you know that rats—"

"I don't want to hear about your dumb, old rats," Lynne interrupted. "Mom sent me to tell you it's time to set the table. It's your turn." She sneezed and grabbed for a tissue. "You're supposed to come right away." Lynne pulled two more tissues from the box and closed the door.

Trish closed the book reluctantly. Learning about rats was much more interesting than she had expected. She left the book on her pillow and went to set the table.

Trish put the last fork in place and hurried to the kitchen. "May I call Sally? The table is all set."

Her mother handed her a big bowl of salad. "It's time for dinner. Put this on the table for me. You can call Sally later."

Trish paused beside the sink, "Mom, did you know that rats—" she began.

"Later, Trish," her mother said. She reached for a potholder and opened the oven door. "I don't have time right now."

A few minutes later Mom called them to the table. Trish bowed her head while Dad asked the blessing. She waited patiently for her turn to share. When it came she turned to Dad.

"I know how to keep the rats from jumping now," she said. "May I take them out of the cage?"

"Please pass the corn," said Lynne.

Dad passed the dish. "How do you keep them from jumping, Trish?"

Trish put down her fork so she could use both hands. "First you pick the rat up in the middle." She scooped up an imaginary rat. "Then you hold it by the base of its tail with your other hand so it can't jump."

"Oh, gross!" Lynne made a face. "How can you touch those scaly things?"

Trish gave her a disgusted look. "Their tails are important. They use them for balance when they jump or climb."

"I don't care what they use their tails for," said Lynne. "Just keep them away from me."

Trish turned back to Dad. "I'm learning all about their habits too. Did you know when they eat they—"

"Please," her mother said, "I know sharing time is supposed to be open to almost any subject, but must you discuss rats at the table?"

Trish picked up her fork. Nobody around here is interested in my pets except Fredrick, she thought. Tomorrow I'll take my book to school and show Sally. She's interested. And just wait until she hears about the babies!

Sally the Brave

The next day after school Trish waited while Sally strapped on her roller skates. "I'm glad you asked your mother if you could come over today," Trish said as they started down the street. "Now we can study the rat book without Herbie pestering us and trying to find out what we're doing."

Sally skated up and down the sidewalk and circled around Trish. "Herbie is a pain, but he's not as bad as one of the boys in the school I used to go to." She skated off again and came back. "Mom said I could stay until four-thirty. We'd better hurry if we want to learn anything about the rats today." She whizzed down the street.

Trish ran to catch up. I wish Sally hadn't worn her skates, she thought. Maybe after she sees the rats she will be so interested she won't want to skate all the time. I can't even talk to her this way.

They reached Trish's apartment building before she spoke again. "I can hardly wait to show you the rats," she said.

Sally clumped up the steps. "I want to see the babies. I've never seen baby rats before."

Trish opened the door, and they went inside. Mrs. Peabody was standing by the elevator with her back to them. "Quick!" Trish whispered, "Let's take the stairs."

Sally rolled to a stop. "Why, is your elevator broken?"

Trish pulled her by the arm. "Hurry up!"

"Wait. I'll have to take off my skates first. It's too hard to climb a lot of stairs with them on."

33

The elevator came down. Mrs. Peabody stepped inside and turned around. When she saw them she held the door open with her cane. "Well, don't just stand there," she said crossly. "I can't wait all day."

Trish sighed. "Now we have to ride up with her," she whispered. They hurried across the hall and stepped into the elevator.

Mrs. Peabody frowned at Sally. "Who are you?" she asked. "Do you live in this building?"

"My name is Sally Santini. I live down the block," she said. "I'm Trish's best friend."

Trish couldn't believe her ears. Mrs. Peabody didn't scare Sally one bit! And she'd said they were best friends! A warm, happy glow started in the middle of Trish's chest and spread all the way to her fingers and toes.

The elevator stopped and the door slid open. The girls waited until Mrs. Peabody got out. She turned and shook her finger at them. "Mind you behave yourselves," she warned. "And don't go skating in the halls." She went on down the hall to her apartment.

Sally waited until Mrs. Peabody's door closed. "Who was that?" she whispered.

"Mrs. Peabody," Trish answered. "She's always asking questions. That's why I wanted to take the stairs." They started down the hall to Trish's apartment.

Trish unlocked the door and led the way to her room. Lynne's side was neat and tidy. Trish glanced at her side of the room. She had forgotten to make her bed again and pick up her clothes. She dropped her books and coat on the chair.

"The rats are over there." Trish pointed to the cage on the shelf. While Sally was busy looking at the rats, Trish pushed her dirty socks and T-shirt under the bed with her foot. Then she quickly pulled the bedspread up over the rumpled blanket. She promised herself she would clean her side of the room properly the minute Sally was gone.

"I don't see any baby rats," said Sally.

Trish hurried over to the cage and lifted off the wire top. "They're in here," she said, as she opened the nesting box.

Mrs. Longtails ran over to the opening of the box and watched them anxiously. "We aren't going to touch your babies," Trish told her. "She might bite us if we do," Trish added as an aside to Sally. "It says so in the book."

Sally peeked into the nesting box and wrinkled up her nose. "I thought the babies would be cute," she said.

Trish caught her lower lip between her teeth. It was true the baby rats were not beautiful. "They will look better when their eyes and ears open," she said hopefully. What if Sally changed her mind and didn't want to learn about the rats after all? Trish put the lid back on the box.

"The rats look almost like newborn kittens, only smaller," said Sally. "Newborn kittens have more hair, but they aren't cute either."

Trish felt limp with relief. Sally liked the little rats after all! Now they were really best friends. She picked up Mr. Longtails. "Would you like to hold him?" she asked.

Sally looked at the rat for a minute, but she didn't hold out her hands. "Are you sure he won't bite?"

"Not if you're gentle. Fredrick holds him all the time."

"Well, I'll take him for a minute." Sally looked nervous as she took the rat. Then she smiled. "Holding him isn't as bad as I thought."

"You want to feed him?" Trish took a piece of apple from the cage and handed it to Sally. "It's fun to watch them eat."

Mr. Longtails sat up and took the apple. He began to nibble. "His paws are just like little hands," said Sally.

"We'd better put him back now," Trish said when Mr. Longtails had finished the apple. She took the rat and put him back in the cage. "Now let's decide which part of the book each of us are going to tell about."

Sally looked around the room. "Where did you put the book?"

Trish hurried across the room and pulled it out from under her coat. She handed it to Sally. "We need pencils and paper." She got them from her desk. Sally flopped down on the rug and opened the book.

Trish stretched out beside her and leaned her chin in her hands.

"You choose first," she said.

Sally looked at the book for a minute. "I'm going to do this one about how they keep themselves clean," she said.

"Then I'll do this one about whiskers," Trish said, pointing to the opposite page.

For the next half hour they read and wrote busily, scrawling the words across their papers. Sally finished first.

"Listen to this," she said. She sat up and picked up her paper. "Rats are very clean," she read. "They spend a lot of time washing themselves after they eat. They do this by licking their paws and rubbing them over their faces and ears."

Trish nodded. "They do that all the time. Fredrick never wants to wait until they've finished to hold them."

"They also tunnel through the shavings on the bottom of their cages," Sally continued. "Cedar shavings are very good for this because they help clean the rat's fur and make it glossy."

"I didn't know that," said Trish. "I thought they just liked to dig tunnels."

"Now let me hear yours," said Sally.

Trish sat up and crossed her legs Indian style. "Mine is about whiskers," she said. "Rats have poor eyesight," she began. "They use their whiskers to help them see. Some of their whiskers grow down past their chin. Others grow out from the sides of their faces. The whiskers are very long. In the dark the rats use their whiskers like radar."

Sally got up and walked over to the cage. She bent down and looked at the two rats. "They really do have long whiskers, don't they?"

Trish got up and looked at the rats too. "I never noticed how long the whiskers were before."

Sally turned and looked at the clock on Trish's desk. "I'd better go," she said. "It's almost four-thirty." She got her coat and put it on. "We can go to my house and work on our report tomorrow after school. Mom already said so."

Trish walked Sally to the door. "See you tomorrow," she said.

As the days passed, the baby rats changed from tiny, pink, wiggling things into little balls of fur. Their ears opened, but their eyes were still closed. Trish and Sally took turns going to each other's apartments after school to work on their papers. Trish liked going to Sally's. She lived on the third floor. No one stopped them in the hall the way Mrs. Peabody did. Sally had a big room all to herself because she didn't have a sister to share it with. Mrs. Santini was nice too. She was always smiling and friendly when they came in from school.

One day at Trish's house, Sally bent over the nesting box and looked at the baby rats. "I hope they come out of there before it's time to take them to school," she said.

Trish opened the book and turned to the chapter about baby rats. "It says they are weaned at two weeks. They must come out of the nesting box to eat after that." Trish frowned. "The babies are almost two weeks old now. Mom and Lynne still don't like Mr. and Mrs. Longtails. I'm afraid they won't like the babies either."

Sally settled herself on the floor and reached for the book. "Maybe if you tell them some of the nice things we've learned about the rats, they will change their minds," she suggested.

"That's a good idea." Trish picked up her pencil and sat down beside Sally. "I'm going to make a list of all the nice things. And tonight I'm going to tell Mom and Lynne all about them."

By the time Sally left, Trish had her list memorized. She hurried to the dining room and set the table without being told. When dinnertime came she could hardly wait for her turn to share.

"That was very interesting," Mom said when Fredrick finished sharing. "Now eat your dinner before it gets cold."

"Did you know that pet rats are descendants of laboratory rats?" Trish asked. "They have never been wild rats at all. That's why they're so friendly."

Lynne sniffled and leaned her head on her hand. "Who cares?" she mumbled. Her eyes were watering, and the end of her nose was red.

Mother looked closely at Lynne and frowned. "You should have been over that cold by now. If it doesn't clear up in the next day or two I'm going to take you to the doctor."

"Maybe it isn't a cold," Dad suggested. "Lynne has had it for over a week. It would be a good idea to have it checked."

Lynne sat up straight and put her hand down. "Oh, Dad, it's only a head cold. I'm all right."

Mom reached over and touched Lynne's forehead with her fingertips. "You don't feel feverish, but you certainly can't study with a stuffy nose and watering eyes. I'm going to make an appointment for you."

"My eyes don't itch and water at school," Lynne insisted. "It only bothers me when I'm home. May I be excused? I'm not very hungry."

When dinner was over Trish helped clear the table. "Did you save anything for the rats?" she asked.

Mother turned from the dishwasher and pointed to a small bowl on the end of the counter. "There are some lettuce and celery scraps and a small piece of carrot. Will that do?"

Trish nodded and picked up the bowl. "Come watch the rats," she pleaded. "They are really cute when they eat."

Mom shook her head. "I'm afraid I don't share your interest in rats, Trish. Run along. And feed them quietly. I think Lynne is lying down."

Trish opened the bedroom door softly. Lynne was curled up on her bed with a box of tissues beside her. She raised up and looked at Trish.

"Are you going to feed those awful things again?" Lynne sneezed and reached for a tissue. She looked worse than she had at dinner.

Trish closed the door. "I won't take them out of their cage," she promised. "But I have to give them their vegetables."

Lynne moaned and pulled the pillow over her head.

It's a Secret

On the way to school the next morning Trish and Sally stopped to gather a big bouquet of autumn leaves for Mrs. Martin. Sally added a large golden maple leaf to the red and yellow leaves in her hand.

"I can't come over today," she said. "My grandparents are coming for a visit. I have to go right home after school."

"We've learned almost everything in the book about rats," Trish said. She scuffed through the leaves looking for another red one. "We will be ready when it's time to take them to school."

Sally examined a green-and-yellow leaf and tossed it aside. "I can hardly wait to see everybody's face when we bring the rats into the room," she said. She looked at Trish and they giggled.

"Me either," Trish agreed. "I bet Barbara will be scared of them. She's afraid of everything, even ants." She held her bouquet of leaves next to Sally's. "Do you think we have enough?" she asked.

Sally looked at the leaves and nodded. "We should have another red one, but we'd better hurry. We're going to be late for school."

"I'll race you!" Trish called and ran down the street.

Sally pounded after her. "Last one to the crosswalk is a slowpoky turtle!" she shouted.

They were still laughing when they hurried down the hall to Mrs. Martin's room.

"I would have won if my legs were longer," Trish panted.

Breathlessly they handed Mrs. Martin the bouquet. "Why, thank you," she said. "What beautiful fall colors." She put them in a big glass jar and set them on her desk. Then she stepped back to admire them. The gold leaves almost matched the dress she was wearing. Trish looked at Sally and grinned.

The bell rang, and the rest of the class came rushing in. Trish and Sally took their seats. When everyone had settled down, Mrs. Martin wrote on the blackboard, MATH page 32.

"This is your assignment for today," she said. "When you have finished, please quietly put your papers on my desk."

Trish got out her math book. It was her hardest subject. But she had to get it right if she wanted to bring the rats to school. Her stomach felt all funny until she looked at Sally in the next aisle. The feeling went away. Now that Sally was going to stand up in front of the class with her, she didn't feel a bit afraid. Sally was the nicest best friend she'd ever had.

When Trish finished her math, she looked at the clock. She was surprised to see that she still had five minutes for free time. She took her paper up to the front of the room and laid it on Mrs. Martin's desk. When she turned around, Sally motioned to her. Trish followed her back to the science table to look at the snakes and toads.

"They're fun to watch," Trish whispered. "But not as much fun as the rats. I wish our science project was over."

Sally nodded. "Me too. Stanley says the snakes and toads will be gone when we come back to school on Tuesday. We have Monday off, remember?"

"Oh good!" Trish clamped her hand over her mouth and remembered to whisper. "The baby rats are sure to be out of the nest by then."

The rest of the day went slowly. Fridays were always the longest day of the week. Trish could hardly wait to get home and see the rats.

When school let out, Trish and Sally started home.

"I can't come over until Monday," Sally said. "My grandparents will be there when I get home."

"But we'll see each other tomorrow at Sabbath School," said Trish. "Maybe our parents will let us sit together in church."

"I don't think so," said Sally. "My grandparents are only going to be here for the weekend. I'd better sit with them."

Trish jumped over a crack in the sidewalk. "Can you come over on Sunday if the baby rats come out?"

Sally leaped over the next crack. "I don't think so. Mom said Grandma made something for me, and I have to try it on to make sure it fits. It might have to be fixed." They took turns jumping the cracks.

"What did she make?" Trish asked as they waited for Mr. Bailey.

"It's a surprise. My grandparents are fun. I'm going to stay home while they are here." Mr. Bailey waved the crowd of children across the street. "See you tomorrow," Sally called when they reached the other side. Trish waved and started home.

Fredrick jumped up the minute Trish came through the door. "I want to see the rats," he said and followed her into her room. He sat down on the floor in front of the cage. "I'm ready to hold Mr. Longtails," he said.

"In a minute," Trish answered. She dropped her things on her chair and walked over to the cage.

Suddenly a tiny brown-and-white rat lurched out of the nesting box. Its eyes were still narrow slits. It stood there for a minute with its legs spread far apart and its tail stuck straight out behind. It looked around. Then with its little tail trembling, the baby rat staggered across the cage toward Trish and Fredrick. It pressed its tiny pink nose against the glass side of the cage and stared at them like a nearsighted gopher.

Mrs. Longtails stopped eating. She dropped the kernel of grain and ran over to the baby rat. She picked it up by the scruff of the neck, like a mother cat carrying a kitten, and carried it back to the nesting box. She went back to the feed dish. But before Mrs. Longtails could eat another kernel of grain the baby rat staggered out of the nest again.

Fredrick rocked back and forth with laughter. "That little mouse is sure nosy!"

"Ssssh, not so loud," Trish whispered. "It's a secret." She smothered her own giggles behind her hand as Mrs. Longtails grabbed up the baby rat again.

"Where did you get it?" Fredrick whispered.

Trish caught her lower lip between her teeth and wondered if she dared tell him. All of the baby rats would be out of the nesting box soon. He would be sure to see them, and he might make a fuss if she tried to keep him out of her room now.

"Promise not to tell?" she asked. Fredrick nodded. "Mr. and Mrs. Longtails have babies," she whispered. "If you won't tell Mom or Lynne or anyone, I'll show them to you."

Fredrick's eyes widened and his mouth fell open. "I promise! Show me!" he cried, jumping to his feet.

"Shhhhhh! Remember it's a secret," she reminded him. Trish took the top off the cage and lifted the lid of the nesting box.

Fredrick peeked inside the box. "Look at all the baby ones!" he cried. "Let me hold one!" His hand was halfway to the box when Trish grabbed him by the sleeve.

"Mrs. Longtails will bite you if you touch them. They're too little to hold." Fredrick's lip began to quiver. "As soon as Mrs. Longtails lets them come out of the nest you can hold one," Trish said quickly.

"Promise?" Fredrick sniffled.

"Promise." Trish put her arm around him. "If you don't cry, I'll let you hold Mr. Longtails right now."

"I'm not crying." Fredrick brushed the back of his hand over his eyes and smiled. He sat down on the floor and looked up at Trish. "I'm ready," he said.

On Sunday morning Trish finished her breakfast and hurried back to her room. She bent over the cage and found all of the baby rats out of the nest. She sat down on the floor and pulled her knees up to her chin. The baby rats' heads looked too big for their bodies, just like the pictures of baby rats in the book. Their eyes were open, but not as wide and round as the big rats' eyes. Their tiny ears were still hairless. They looked like little pink rose petals. Some of the babies were hooded rats, like Mrs. Longtails. Their heads and shoulders were brown or black, and the rest of their bodies were white. One little rat was black like Mr. Longtails. And he had the same white markings on his feet and tail. Trish wondered why they were called Irish black rats when they had white on them too.

The door opened and Fredrick poked his head into the room. "I want—" His eyes grew big and he grinned. "They're out!" he shouted. "I get to hold one!"

Trish's finger flew to her lips. "Shhhh! Be quiet and shut the door."

Fredrick clamped his hand over his mouth and closed the door quietly. He tiptoed over to the cage. "Let me hold one," he whispered. "You promised I could."

"I want to count them first," Trish said.

"There's Nosy!" Fredrick pressed his finger against the glass and pointed to the little rat in the corner.

Trish laughed. "That's a good name for him." She counted quickly. "Eight. There are eight babies."

A little black-and-white rat leaped from the top of the nesting box and landed near the feed dish. Fredrick knelt beside the cage and giggled. "Did you see him? I'm going to call him Jumper."

"I get to name some of them too," Trish said. A little brown-and-white rat crept close to the side of the cage, brushing its whiskers along the glass. "Hi, Whiskers," Trish said. The baby rat turned his head and looked at Trish as though he knew his name already.

The little black rat burrowed through the shavings and came up on the other side of the cage. Fredrick named him Digger. He pointed to a dark-brown-and-white rat. "We can call that one Mrs. Longtails. It looks just like its mom."

"It's a boy rat," Trish said. She thought for a minute. "His eyes are open wider than the other baby rats' eyes. They're round and shiny just like the buttons on Mom's favorite blouse. Let's call him Buttons."

Across the cage a little black-and-white rat crept up behind Nosy. It stole the piece of apple Nosy had been eating and scurried off into the corner with his loot. Trish laughed. "We'll call that one Bandit," she said.

"It's my turn," Fredrick said. "I get to name the next one."

There were only two rats left to name. One had a dark-brown patch on his back. Fredrick named him Spot. Trish had never heard of a rat being called Spot before. But she couldn't think of a better name. The last little rat was the smallest of the litter. The fur on her head and shoulders was much lighter than the other rats' fur.

"I'm going to call the little one Taffy," Trish said.

Fredrick sat down on the floor. "I want to hold Nosy now." He held out his hands and waited.

Trish reached into the cage. This time Mrs. Longtails didn't seem to mind. Trish picked up the baby rat and handed him to Fredrick. "Don't squeeze him," she warned. "Remember, he's still a baby."

Nosy lifted his head and wiggled his whiskers as he sat up in Fredrick's hand. Then he scampered up the front of Fredrick's shirt and disappeared into his pocket. A moment later Nosy popped his head out and nibbled on the M&M he had found. Fredrick laughed so hard he almost fell over backwards.

Trish looked up as the door opened. She had forgotten all about Lynne's being home. She was always off somewhere with Deb at this time on Sundays. But today she had to stay home because of her cold.

"Mice too!" Lynne gasped.

"They're baby rats!" Fredrick announced happily. He scooped Nosy out of his pocket. "You want to hold one?"

Lynne backed toward the door. "You keep that thing away from me!" she shrieked. "Mother!"

Trish leaped to her feet. "Be quiet!" she said. But it was too late. She could hear Mother coming down the hall.

"What is going on in here?" Mother wanted to know.

"Look!" Lynne pointed to the cage and sneezed.

Mother's eyes widened. She put her hands on her hips and tapped her toe. "Patricia, I agreed to two rats. Not a whole army of mice. I don't care where they came from. I want you to get rid of those things at once."

Trish put her hands behind her back and dug her toe into the carpet. "I can't. Mrs. Longtails had babies."

Mother threw her hands in the air. "I might have known." She stepped closer to the cage and looked inside. "How many are there?"

"Eight," Trish answered in a soft voice.

"As soon as they are old enough, you will have to give some of them away. Two rats are more than enough around here. And ten are certainly more than I bargained for," her mother said.

"But, Mom, can't I just keep part of them?" Trish pleaded.

"If you had your way, this whole room would be full of rats," Lynne complained. She sneezed three times. "I can't even enjoy reading in my own room anymore." She grabbed up her book and a box of tissues and stalked out the door.

"Lynne is right," Mom said. "Those little ones will soon be full grown. You can't keep them all in such a small cage."

"But can't I—" Trish began.

Mother held up her hand. "No more arguments, Trish." She turned on her heel and left the room.

As soon as Mom closed the door, Trish turned and looked at the baby rats again. "They are all so cute. I don't want to give any of them away."

"You can't give my Nosy away," Fredrick protested. He held the little rat close to his chest.

"I'm not going to give him away. Put him back in the cage now. I'll think of some way to keep them," Trish promised.

More Room

Trish was glad they had the day off from school on Monday. She decided on a plan as she cleaned her half of the bedroom.

I get my allowance today, she thought. With the money I have saved I can buy a bigger cage. Then Mom won't make me give any of the little rats away.

She straightened her sheets and blankets and pulled up the bedspread. She dug the dirty clothes out from under her bed and carried them down the hall to the laundry hamper. Then she sorted through the box she found under her bed.

Trish pounced on the dust-covered book in the middle of the box. "Now I can find out how it ends." She settled her back against the bed and stretched her legs out in front of her.

Trish had read half a page when the soft rustling noises coming from the cage reminded her of the rats. Reluctantly she closed the book and put it on top of her desk. She gathered up the rest of the trash. Then she picked up the wastebasket and stepped back to admire her side of the room.

"Now Lynne doesn't have anything to complain about. My half of the room looks as good as hers." Trish turned to look at Lynne's side and stopped to stare.

Lynne's slippers were in the middle of the floor. Her robe was draped over the chair, and her bed hadn't been made! That wasn't like Lynne at all.

Suddenly Trish had an idea. She set the wastebasket by the door and gathered up Lynne's things. She put the slippers neatly under the bed and went to hang Lynne's robe in the closet. She hit her bare toe hard against Lynne's roller skate as she reached for a hanger. Trish sat down quickly on the floor and grabbed her toe. When the pain eased she wiggled her toe carefully.

"I guess it isn't broken." She reached over and gave the roller skate a hard push. "How can Lynne and Sally wear those things? I don't see how they keep from falling and breaking all of their bones." Then she put on her shoes and socks and hung up Lynne's robe.

When she finished making Lynne's bed, she looked around. Everything looked neat and clean and ready for Mom to vacuum. She gave Lynne's pink bedspread one last pat. "There. Now maybe Lynne won't mind a bigger cage of rats being in here." She took the money from her top drawer and picked up her wastebasket.

Trish found her mother in the kitchen taking the breakfast dishes out of the dishwasher. "May I have my allowance now?" she asked. "I cleaned my room."

Mother put the glasses in the cupboard and turned around. "Are you sure your room is really clean? Did you clean under the bed?"

Trish nodded. "I even cleaned Lynne's half of the room too."

"That was nice of you, Trish. Lynne isn't feeling well at all."

"Please may I have my allowance?" Trish asked again. "I want to go to the store."

"You can't go now," her mother said. "Lynne has an appointment with Dr. Wright at ten. We have to leave in a few minutes."

"Why do I have to go? Why can't I stay here with Dad?" Trish asked over the clatter of the dishes.

"Your father had to go back to the office this morning. I'm sorry, Trish. You'll just have to come with us."

This would be a perfect time to get the bigger cage and bring it home. Then when Mom got back she could see how much room the rats had, and she wouldn't make a fuss about giving them away. "I could stay here by myself when I got back from the store. I'm not a baby anymore."

Mother stacked the last bowl in place and closed the cupboard door. "Well, I suppose you could," she admitted. "Dr. Wright's office is only three blocks away. It shouldn't take too long. Lynne is his first patient. Bring me my purse. It's in the living room."

"Thanks, Mom!" Trish cried and ran to get her mother's purse.

Lynne was sprawled on the sofa with a box of tissues beside her. Her eyes were red and puffy, and her nose was redder than it had been before she got dressed.

"I'm sorry you don't feel good," Trish said. "I cleaned your half of the room and made your bed."

Lynne sniffled and dug her knuckle into her left eye. "Thanks," she said.

Trish picked up her mother's purse and started back to the kitchen. Lynne must really be sick, she thought. She didn't yell about my touching her things or go inspect the room or anything.

Her mother counted out the change and handed it to Trish. "Be sure you come straight home," she said. "And wear your boots and raincoat; it's beginning to rain."

"Aw, Mom," Trish moaned. She hated wearing her rain boots, but she went to get them. This was no time to argue. Mom might not let her go to the store.

They all rode down in the elevator together. Trish turned at the corner, while her mother and Lynne and Fredrick went on down the street. It was raining hard by the time Trish reached the store. She ducked inside, glad that she had worn her boots.

Trish went straight to the pet section and looked around for Miss Forrest. She found her filling the bird feeders.

Miss Forrest smiled when she saw Trish. "Back so soon?" she said."Your rats must be big eaters."

Trish smiled and shook her head. "I came to buy a bigger cage this time. Mrs. Longtails has eight babies, and they need more room."

"I'll show you what we have." Miss Forrest led Trish past the dog collars and chew-bones to the shelves filled with cages and fish tanks. There were all sizes and shapes. "Which one would you like?" Miss Forrest asked.

Trish looked at the long row of glass cages. "That one," she said, pointing to the largest one. There was sure to be enough room for all of the rats in that.

Miss Forrest laughed. "My goodness, you must be planning to raise rats like my Aunt Amelia. She started out with one pair too. Now she has dozens and dozens of rats."

Trish tried to imagine dozens of rats in cages on her side of the room. That would really make Mom and Lynne mad. "Oh no," Trish said. "I only want to keep the ones I have now. Your aunt must like them a lot to have so many pets."

"Aunt Amelia doesn't raise them as pets," Miss Forrest explained. "She raises them for pet shops and takes orders for rats of unusual colors." She looked at the cage Trish had chosen. "If you don't plan to raise rats, you won't want to spend your money on such a large cage. What size cage do you have now?"

Trish pointed to one of the small cages. "It's only that big."

Miss Forrest nodded. "If you don't want to raise any more rats you will want to separate some of them. You can still use the cage you have. The rest will fit very nicely into one of the medium-sized cages, there on the middle shelf. They are only $10.95."

Trish put her hands behind her back and looked down at her shoes. "I guess I can't buy one today after all. I don't have that much money."

"That's all right." Miss Forrest smiled. "We always have those cages in stock. You can buy one anytime." She went to help an impatient-looking woman standing by the tanks of goldfish.

It will take forever to save up enough for a big cage, Trish thought, as she walked back to the front of the store. "I only have $2.50, and I only get 75 cents a week." Trish counted on her fingers. "It will take ten weeks to save that much, and I still have to buy the rat food. The baby rats will be grown before I can buy a bigger cage."

She stopped at the counter and bought a small bag of popcorn. It didn't matter now if she saved her money.

"Hi, Trish," Sally called.

Trish turned around. She finally saw Sally standing in front of a display of roller skates. She had on her boots and raincoat too. "Hi!" Trish called and rushed over to join Sally. "What are you doing here? I thought you had to stay home all weekend."

"I came to buy a spool of blue thread for my grandmother." Sally picked up one of the roller skates and spun the wide yellow wheels. "These are almost like mine. I wish you had a pair; then we could skate together."

"What did your grandmother make for you?" Trish asked quickly to change the subject.

Sally put the roller skate down and reached into her pocket. "A really neat blue dress. This is a scrap of the material. Don't you love the little pink flowers on it?" Trish looked at it and nodded. "What are you doing here?" Sally asked.

"Oh, I almost forgot to tell you! The baby rats came out of the nest. There are eight of them."

"Oh, I wish I could come and see them," Sally moaned. "But Mom told me to come right back. Was your Mom mad when she found out about the babies?"

Trish rolled her eyes and nodded. "I'll say! Mom said I can't keep them because the cage is too small. I came to buy a bigger one, but I don't have enough money."

"What are you going to do?" Sally asked.

Trish shrugged. "I don't know. I have to think of something else. They're all so cute; I don't want to give any of them away. Besides it's almost time to take them to school."

"I have to go," Sally said. Trish walked over to the counter with her and waited while Sally paid for the thread. "I'll ask my mom if I can have one of the rats," Sally said. "Then if you have to give them away, you can always come over and see mine." She giggled. "I'll have to wait until my grandparents leave. I don't think my grandmother would like the idea of having a rat at our house. She might talk Mom out of it."

They left the store together and splashed in all the puddles on the way back to the corner. Trish stamped down hard in the biggest puddle. A lady with a yellow umbrella gasped as the water splashed up onto her stockings. She turned and glared at Trish.

"Sorry," Trish mumbled in a small, embarrassed voice.

Sally stopped when they reached the corner. "Maybe when Stanley sees the little rats he will want some too. He's always doing stuff with animals. Then maybe you could go and visit them too."

"That's a good idea," Trish agreed. "If I can't think of a way to keep all of them, I wouldn't mind so much giving them to Stanley. He would take good care of them."

"I'll see you tomorrow," Sally called. "I hope you think of something." She rushed off down the street.

Trish felt better as she rode up in the elevator. Maybe by tomorrow I'll think of a way to keep all of the babies, she thought. The elevator door slid open. Trish pulled the chain that held her key out of the neck of her shirt and stepped out into the hall. By the time she reached her apartment, Mrs. Peabody's door had opened and the old lady was starting down the hall. Trish hurried to get the key in the lock, hoping she could get inside before Mrs. Peabody could speak to her.

"Did you wipe your feet when you came in?" Mrs. Peabody asked. She tapped her cane against the hall carpet.

"Yes, ma'am," Trish said politely. She twisted the key in the lock and shoved the door open and rushed inside. "Why does that old Mrs. Peabody have to live on our floor anyway?" She pulled off her boots and raincoat and hung her coat up to dry. Then she took her bag of popcorn and went to play with the little rats before Lynne came home.

Mrs. Longtails was taking a nap on top of the nesting box. The baby rats were climbing all over Mr. Longtails, biting him on the tail and chewing on his ears. Trish laughed. They play just like puppies, she thought. She poked a kernel of popcorn through the wire mesh on top of the cage. Nosy got to it first. He snatched it up and ran to the corner. Bandit, true to his name, followed and tried to steal the popcorn away from Nosy. But Nosy turned his face to the corner and kept on eating.

"Would you all like some?" Trish asked. She opened the top of the cage and poured some of the popcorn inside. The little rats swarmed over the fluffy, white kernels, scrambling for their share. Mrs. Longtails woke up and came to join in the feast.

Hearing the front door close, Trish dropped the sack of

popcorn on her bed and went into the living room. Lynne was already talking to Deb on the phone when she came down the hall.

"Did the doctor give Lynne something for her cold?" Trish asked Mother.

Mother sighed and sank down in her easy chair. "Lynne doesn't have a cold. She has an allergy."

"What's an allergy?" Trish asked. It sounded like a terrible disease to have. "How did she catch it?"

Mother smiled. "An allergy isn't contagious. Lynne is sensitive to something she has come in contact with. That's what causes her to sneeze and her eyes to itch and water. Dr. Wright is running some tests to find out what it is. We will know in a few days."

Narrow Escape

Sally came home with Trish after school Tuesday. They went straight to Trish's room to see the baby rats.

"Mom was right about the cage being too small," Trish admitted. "Now that the babies are out all of the time, there isn't much room for them."

Sally bent over the cage. "Aren't they cute! I don't blame you for wanting to keep them. Why don't you ask your dad to buy a bigger cage for them?"

Trish shook her head. "I promised to take care of the rats all by myself. Besides, he agrees with Mom. He says I should give some of the rats away."

Sally knelt beside the cage and watched the rats. "May I pick out the one I want now?" she asked. "I want to hold it."

"You can have any one you want except Nosy. Fredrick wants to keep him." She crouched beside Sally and pointed to the little brown-and-white rat. "That's Nosy over there, the one by the feed dish eating the lettuce."

Sally puckered up her mouth and frowned. "It's hard to choose. I like them all." Suddenly she laughed and pointed. "That's the one I want, the one biting Mrs. Longtails on the ear."

"I named that one Taffy," Trish said. "But you can change her name if you want."

"No, I like that name. May I hold her now?"

Trish reached in the cage and caught the little rat. "What did your mother say when you asked if you could have one?" She handed Taffy to Sally.

"I didn't have a chance to ask her all weekend. My grandparents were still there when I left this morning. Their plane didn't leave until noon." Taffy ran up Sally's arm and tried to hide in the bend of her elbow. Sally tucked her arm close to her side and laughed. "Help me quick! She's tickling me!"

Trish laughed and reached around behind Sally. She caught Taffy as she wiggled past Sally's arm. "You'd better hold her by the tail like the book says," Trish suggested when Taffy was safely cupped in Sally's hands again.

"I have an idea," said Sally. "Why don't we take Taffy over to my house and show her to my Mom. Then she can see how cute and friendly Taffy is. I know she will let me keep her."

"I'll go ask Mom if I can go with you." Sally started to get up. "You'd better stay here. Mom won't let me bring the rats out of my room. You can feed Taffy some carrot while I'm gone. There's some in that plastic bag by the cage." Trish hurried out the door.

Trish found her mother in Fredrick's room with a cleaning cloth in her hand. "I gave Sally one of my rats," she said. "She wants to take it home to show her mother. May I go with her?"

As Mother turned around to answer, Fredrick picked up the bottle of window cleaner. He sprayed the crayon picture he had drawn on the window glass until the cleaner ran down in a puddle on the windowsill. "Oh, Fredrick!" Mother took the spray bottle away from him and handed him a paper towel. "You may go, Trish, but don't stay too long. We're having an early dinner tonight, and I want you to set the table."

"But it's Lynne's turn," Trish protested.

"I know. She isn't feeling well, Trish. She can take a turn for you when she's well again."

"OK," Trish agreed. "I'll be back in half an hour." She hurried back to her room.

"I can go," she said, and reached for her coat.

"I need something to carry Taffy in," Sally said. "She keeps trying to climb up my arm, and I'm afraid I'll hurt her if I keep holding onto her tail."

"I think there's a box in the closet," Trish said. She opened the closet door and looked up on her side of the closet shelf.

Sally walked over and stood beside her. "I don't see an empty one," Trish said. "All of those boxes have games in them."

"There's one." Sally pointed to Lynne's side of the shelf. "Is it empty?"

Trish looked at the box. It had been there for a long time. Lynne got mad if she touched anything on her side of the closet. But this was an emergency. Maybe she won't miss it if I bring it right back, she thought. "It's kind of big for one rat," said Trish as she got the box down. She pulled off the lid and poured shavings into the bottom of the box. "I'll get some feed for you too. Do you want to keep Taffy at your house today if your mother says it's all right?"

Sally didn't say anything. She was still standing by the closet door looking at something on the floor inside.

"Are you sure Taffy is the one you want? You can have a different one."

Sally shook her head. "Taffy is OK." She put the baby rat in the box and closed the lid. "Let's go." Sally carried the box all the way home without saying a word.

Muffin, Sally's cat, ran out into the hall to meet them when Sally opened the door. He purred and walked between Sally's feet, the way he always did when he wanted her to pick him up. "Oh Muffin, stop that!" Sally snapped. "You're such a pest sometimes." She moved him out of the way with her foot and stalked down the hall.

Trish stared after her as she disappeared around the corner into the living room. Sally sure is acting funny, she thought. I've never heard her speak crossly to Muffin before. Trish bent down and stroked Muffin's long white fur, then followed Sally into the living room.

Sally had the box open and was holding it out so that Mrs. Santini could look inside. "Please, may I keep it?" she asked.

Mrs. Santini turned reluctantly from the television program she was watching and glanced in the box. "Good heavens, Sally! What is that thing?"

"A baby rat," Sally answered. "Trish has a whole family of them. Can I keep her? I'll put her in that tank my goldfish were in."

"Well," Mrs. Santini said slowly, "I suppose so. If you keep it in the tank. I don't want it running around the apartment." She glanced back at the television and picked up her pen. "The tank is in the storage closet at the end of the hall. I'll get it down for you as soon as I finish taking down this recipe."

"I can get it," Sally said. Trish followed her back out into the hall. Sally put the box on the floor and opened the closet door. "There it is," she said, "on that top shelf."

"I'll help you get it down," Trish offered. She stood on her tiptoes and reached for the tank. "What happened to your goldfish? Did they die?"

"Sort of," Sally mumbled. She pulled the tank to the edge of the shelf.

"What do you mean, sort of?" Trish asked. She inched the tank a little farther off the shelf.

"Muffin ate them."

Trish turned to stare at Sally. "Muffin *ate* them?" The cat heard his name and came running. He rubbed against Trish's legs and began to purr.

Sally shrugged. "He got the cover off the tank and caught the fish with his paws."

Trish stepped back and Muffin moved away. "Cats like rats as much as they do fish," she said. She looked down at the box. The lid was partway off. Trish gasped. She reached down and snatched the lid from the box.

"What's the matter?" Sally asked, turning around and looking down at Trish.

"Taffy's gone!" Trish wailed.

"She must be here in the hall," Sally said. "She didn't have time to go very far." They looked up and down the hall.

You mean she didn't have a chance to go very far, Trish thought, as she watched Muffin washing his face. "Don't you think Muffin looks fatter?" she asked suspiciously.

"No, I don't think so," Sally said. Then she snatched the big white cat up in her arms. He draped himself over her shoulder and purred contentedly. "Do you think Muffin ate Taffy?" she demanded crossly.

"Well, he could have."

Sally glared at Trish. "Muffin wouldn't eat anything as gross as a rat! He's a civilized cat."

"He ate your fish," Trish reminded her hotly.

Muffin cocked his ears forward and stared at something in the closet. His muscles bunched as he put his front paws on Sally's shoulder. Trish turned to look too. Something moved on the bottom shelf. Trish caught a glimpse of Taffy.

"There she is!" Trish cried. "Don't let go of Muffin." She got down on her hands and knees. Taffy crept behind a clear glass vase and sat very still. Trish reached around both sides of the vase, moving slowly so she wouldn't frighten Taffy even more. Taffy backed up when she saw Trish's hand coming toward her. "I got her!" Trish cried triumphantly. Taffy's little heart beat wildly as she cuddled against Trish's hands.

Muffin's big yellow eyes followed Trish's every move as she put Taffy back in the box and closed the lid. "Don't you think you should put Muffin in the kitchen until we get Taffy in the cage and fasten the lid on good and tight? I think he wants to eat her."

Sally's face turned pink as she held tight to the struggling cat. "I don't want your dumb old rat anyway," she shouted. She jerked the door of her room open. "And I don't want to be your friend anymore. So just take your rat and go home!" she cried and slammed the door.

Sally should have known that rotten old cat would try to eat Taffy, Trish thought as she let herself out. I don't care if she is mad at me. I'm glad poor little Taffy didn't end up being a cat's dinner. She clutched the box tight and hurried home.

Lynne was lying on the sofa when Trish came in. Trish remembered the box and hurried to put Taffy back in the cage before Lynne noticed it.

I don't know what Sally has to be mad about, she thought. Muffin wanted to catch Taffy the minute he saw her. It's a good thing Sally didn't want to keep her. Muffin would have tried to eat her first chance he got. She emptied the shavings out of the box and started to put it back on Lynne's side of the shelf. Lynne's roller skates were sitting right there in plain sight when Trish opened the closet door. Trish caught her lower lip between her teeth. "I bet Sally thought they were mine," she said out loud. "No wonder she acted so funny on the way to her house. It wasn't just Muffin and Taffy she was mad about; it was the roller skates. I'm going to call her right away and tell her they're not mine." She rushed down the hall to the telephone.

"Time to set the table, Trish," her mother called.

"I want to call Sally first," Trish answered. "It's important."

"You just came back from Sally's. You can call her after dinner. I'm sure your news can wait until then. Hurry now, dinner is almost ready."

Trish hung up the phone and went to set the table.

All through dinner Trish wondered if Sally would understand about the roller skates. She shook her head when Dad asked if she had anything to share. She cleaned her plate and gulped down her milk. "May I be excused?" she asked.

"Is that all you're going to eat?" Dad asked. "No dessert either?"

"I'm not very hungry," Trish said. "May I go now?"

Dad nodded "We're having apple pie. Sure you won't change your mind?"

Trish hesitated for a second. Apple pie was her favorite dessert, but it was more important to call Sally. "No thanks." She jumped up from the table and hurried to the phone. She dialed Sally's number and let it ring a long time. There was no answer.

Trish went to her room and picked up her rat book. She sat down at her desk and turned the pages slowly. I should have told Sally before that I'm afraid to roller-skate, she thought, instead of telling her that I don't have any. Now she thinks I lied to her, and I didn't. Not really. I just didn't tell her everything. I should have told her. She's my very best friend, and you're supposed to tell best friends all of your secrets. I'm going to tell her tomorrow morning, first thing.

"May I hold Nosy?"

Trish looked up. Fredrick was standing in the doorway with his hands in his pockets.

"Is dinner over?" she asked.

Fredrick nodded. "I ate all of my pie. It was good. May I hold Nosy now?"

"Not right now. I have to go help Mom with the dishes. You can hold him when I get through." Fredrick looked so disappointed Trish almost changed her mind. "You can come in and watch the rats while I'm gone. I'll take Nosy out for you when I get back." Fredrick was leaning over the cage when Trish left the room.

Mother had picked up the dirty dishes by the time Trish came into the kitchen. "Finish clearing the table; I'll do the dishes tonight," she said.

"I don't mind helping," Trish answered. "I don't have anything else to do."

When the dishes were finished Trish started back to her room. She could hear Fredrick laughing before she opened the door.

"Look what Nosy can do," Fredrick shouted. "I taught him all by myself." He pushed the top of the cage back and held a piece of apple just above the narrow opening. Nosy leaped to the rim of the cage and scampered into Fredrick's hand. "Did you see him?" Three more baby rats leaped out of the cage before Trish could cross the room.

"Stop that," she shouted. "You're letting all of the rats out!" She closed the door quickly and ran to the cage. She caught Whiskers and Spot before they got off of her shelf, but Bandit got away.

"Now look what you've done!" Trish put the little rats back in the cage and closed the top. She turned in time to see Bandit scurry under her bed. Trish crawled under after him. He scampered out the other side before she could catch him.

"There he goes!" Fredrick shouted.

Trish wiggled out backward from under the bed. "Where?"

"He ran away," Fredrick said and petted Nosy.

Trish got down on her hands and knees and looked under Lynne's bed. She looked under the drapes and in the closet. Bandit flashed past just out of reach and ran under the dresser. Trish lay down on her stomach and reached under the dresser, feeling around.

"Watch and see if he comes out," she said. She ran her arm under the dresser again.

"He didn't come out," Fredrick said when she stood up.

"I know. Because he wasn't under there," Trish said. "Now help me find him. If he gets out into the living room Mom will really be mad."

Trish spent the next half hour hunting for Bandit. She caught sight of him at last halfway up the drape. She grabbed the little rat and put him back into the cage. Then turned to Fredrick.

"Don't you ever do that again," she scolded as she pushed the top of the cage down hard.

Fredrick wasn't listening. He was too busy playing with Nosy.

The Big Day

Trish ran all the way to the school crossing the next morning. I wish I had remembered to call Sally again last night before it was too late, she thought. I hope she will understand when I tell her about the roller skates.

The curb was crowded with children waiting for Mr. Bailey to let them cross. Trish stepped aside as two first-grade boys pushed each other. She looked down the street. Mr. Bailey stopped the cars. The other children started across. Trish hesitated.

"No use waiting for Sally today, Trish," Mr. Bailey called. "She was the first one across this morning. Said she had to see somebody about going roller-skating after school."

Trish stepped off the curb. "Thanks, Mr. Bailey," she said.

"Don't you go poking along now," Mr. Bailey said as she passed him. "Or you'll be late."

"I don't care if I am late," Trish mumbled. She jammed her hands into her coat pockets and walked along slowly. Sally must really be mad at me. She kicked at the soggy leaves along the sidewalk. Then, balancing herself carefully, she placed one foot in front of the other and walked along the edge of the sidewalk. It wasn't all my fault, she thought. Sally shouldn't have said she would take Taffy in the first place. She wouldn't have seen Lynne's dumb old roller skates if she hadn't needed a box to put Taffy in.

Trish was still half a block from school when she heard the warning bell ring. She ran the rest of the way. Everyone was in their seats when Trish rushed into the room. Mrs. Martin had started to call the role by the time she hung up her coat and sat down.

Trish glanced over at Sally. If I smile at her, she thought, Sally will know I still want to be friends. But Sally didn't look up or turn her head toward Trish at all. Why did I have to be late today? Trish thought. Now I will have to wait until recess to talk to Sally.

"Please open your books to page 48," Mrs. Martin said. Trish glanced once more at Sally and got out her book.

When recess came Trish got up and started toward Sally. Before she could get past Herbie and Bruce, Sally linked her arm through Cindy's, and they left the room. Cindy was best friends with Angela, but she was still absent today. Trish pushed past the boys and started to follow Sally outside.

"Trish, may I see you for a moment," Mrs. Martin called. Reluctantly, Trish turned toward the teacher's desk. Mrs. Martin waited until everyone else had left the room. "I noticed you didn't bring your pets this morning, Trish," she said in a low voice. She opened the schedule book and tapped the red circle around the date with the point of her pencil. "Did you forget today is the big day?"

Trish's mouth went dry. She turned to look at the date on the calendar beside the chalkboard. It was a big black fifteen. If only I had remembered yesterday, Trish thought. I can't get up in front of the whole class and tell about the rats all by myself. What am I going to do? Suddenly she had an idea. Mom and Lynne didn't like the rats. Maybe Mrs. Martin wouldn't like them either. "I have ten rats now," Trish said. "Mrs. Longtails had babies." She watched Mrs. Martin's face hopefully.

Mrs. Martin smiled. "How exciting!" She said. "How old are they?"

"Almost three weeks," Trish answered. If she could make them sound awful enough maybe Mrs. Martin wouldn't want her to bring them at all. "They are all out of the nesting box now, and they crawl all over the cage." Mrs. Martin was still smiling. "Do you still want me to bring them?"

"Of course," Mrs. Martin assured her. "It will be a wonderful learning experience for the whole class."

Trish sighed. "I'll bring them tomorrow," she said.

Mrs. Martin's smile disappeared. "Isn't your mother bringing them this afternoon?"

Trish shook her head. "Mom doesn't like the rats very much."

Two little frown lines appeared on Mrs. Martin's forehead. "I've planned our science period around them today. Could you go home at lunchtime and get them?"

"I guess so," Trish said.

Mrs. Martin smiled again. "That's fine. I'll be looking forward to hearing all about them after our math test this afternoon."

"But what about the snakes and toads?" Trish asked, relieved that she had remembered them in time. "We can't bring pets with live things in the room."

"The janitor took them down to Mrs. Thornby's second-grade class this morning. My classes seemed to be getting a bit bored with them," Mrs. Martin said. "And we finished that unit on Friday. Remember?" Trish turned to look at the science table. It was empty. "Run along outside now."

Trish rushed out of the room. If I can only find Sally and make up with her, she thought, everything will be all right. She saw Sally and Cindy still arm in arm, walking around the playground. She walked slowly toward them, hoping Sally would speak to her.

". . . and she told me she didn't have any roller skates," Trish heard Sally saying. "Then I found out she had a pair all the time."

"I don't blame you for being mad at her," Cindy agreed. They turned around to walk back the way they had come.

Trish stopped too. Her cheeks felt hot when Sally looked around and saw her. Now Sally will think I have been spying on them, she thought.

"Some people don't like their best friends well enough to skate with them," Sally said, looking straight at Trish. Then she stuck her nose in the air and walked away with Cindy.

Trish forgot all about the rats and hurried back to the classroom. Sally didn't even give me a chance to explain, she thought bitterly. Trish squared her shoulders and lifted her chin. All right for you, Sally Santini! she thought. I'm never going to be best friends with you ever again!

The bell rang and the rest of the class came rushing back into the room. Trish passed Mrs. Martin's desk on the way to her seat. Mrs. Martin glanced up and gave her a little secret kind of smile. Trish felt worse than ever. Now she would really have to tell about the rats all by herself.

The rest of the morning flew by. Each time Trish looked up at the clock the minute hand had leaped ahead several minutes. Time had never gone by so fast before. Whenever she wanted it to go by in a hurry, the hands on the clock never seemed to move at all. Trish sighed and tried not to think about that afternoon.

The lunch bell rang much too soon. Trish started home. Why did I tell Mrs. Martin I would bring the rats? Why didn't I just say, "No, I'm sorry. I can't bring them today"? All the way home she tried to think of a good excuse not to go back to school. I could tell Mom I'm sick. Trish shook her head. No, that would never work. Mom always knows when I'm really sick and when I'm just pretending. She climbed the steps to the apartment building and rode up in the elevator. I could tell Mrs. Martin someone stole the rats, she thought. No, she might call Mom. The elevator opened. Trish got out and started down the hall.

Mom was standing in front of their door, talking to Mrs. Peabody. "Why Trish, what are you doing home?" Mrs. Peabody went on down the hall to her own apartment.

"I came home to get the rats," Trish answered, wishing she had said that she was sick instead.

"You don't sound very excited about it," her mother said as they went inside. "I thought you and Sally could hardly wait to take them to school."

"Sally isn't going to help me tell about the rats. She's mad at me; now I have to tell about them all by myself." She turned quickly to mother, "Please, Mom, do I have to go back to school today?" she pleaded.

Mom put her arms around Trish's shoulders and smiled, "Why, Trish, what a thing to say. Of course you have to go back to school." She gave Trish a hug. "You're going to do just fine. Now stop worrying about it and go wash your face and hands while I fix you some lunch."

"I'm not hungry," Trish said. "If I eat anything I might get sick." She started into her room.

Fredrick followed along behind her. "I want to come to school and tell about the rats with you," he said. "I want to tell about my Nosy. He can do tricks."

"You're too little to go to school," Trish said crossly. She picked up the cage and carried it into the living room.

"That cage might get heavy before you get to school," Mother said. "Would you like me to come along and help you with it?"

Trish shook her head. "I can carry it by myself. It's only three blocks to school."

Mother looked relieved. "Well, If you're sure—"

"I'm sure," Trish said.

"I want to go," Fredrick pouted. "I want to go with my Nosy."

"Not today, dear," Mother said. "You can push the elevator button for Trish." Fredrick ran out into the hall. Pushing elevator buttons was one of the things he liked to do best. Trish wished he was old enough to go to school when she stepped into the elevator. Frederick wouldn't mind standing up in front of the room and telling about the rats one little bit.

The cage grew heavier as Trish trudged along. I wish Sally were here, she thought. Maybe when she sees the rats she will talk to me again.

"Whatcha got?" Herbie demanded when Trish carried the cage into Mrs. Martin's room.

"None of your business, Herbie Fletcher," Trish answered as she put the cage down on the science table.

Herbie leaned over her shoulder and peeked into the cage. "Rats!" he announced loudly. "Trish's got rats!" The children crowded around the table. "Let me hold one," Herbie said, reaching for the top of the cage.

Trish threw herself in front of the cage and spread her arms wide. "You leave them alone, Herbie Fletcher!"

"Aw, I'm not going to hurt your old rats," Herbie said. "I just want to hold one."

"Well you can't!" Trish pushed his hand away from the cage. "Don't you dare touch them."

The bell rang. Mrs. Martin tapped her desk with a ruler. "You people in the back of the room take your seats. You will hear all about Trish's pets this afternoon during science period." The other children drifted back to their desks. Herbie crossed his eyes and made a face at Trish as he slid into his seat. Reluctantly Trish walked down the aisle to her own desk. She wished Herbie sat clear across the room, instead of so close to the science table.

Trish stole a glance at Sally. Now that the rats were really here, she still might want to tell about them. She saw Cindy tap Sally on the back and whisper something to Sally. They both looked back at the science table. Sally shook her head; then she leaned over and whispered something to Cindy.

They are talking about me, Trish thought. She put her chin in her hands and wondered what to do now. She sat there for a long time before she remembered the papers they had worked so hard on. That's what I'll do! I can read the papers to the class and not have to look up at all. Then I won't be so scared. A feeling of relief washed over her as she searched through her desk. She turned to look back at the science table, but there was nothing there except the cage of rats. What did I do with them? They have to be here somewhere. Then she remembered.

Trish slumped back in her seat. She had been so worried about bringing the rats she had forgotten all about the papers and her book. They were still on her desk at home.

Trouble With Longtails

Trish got out a clean sheet of paper. I'll write down everything I learned about the rats, she decided. Then I can still read it without looking at the class. She wrote her name at the top of the paper and printed RATS neatly above the top line. She chewed the eraser of her pencil and stared at the paper for a long time. She looked back at the rats, then over at Sally. Nothing seemed to help. She couldn't remember anything about the rats. All she could think of was standing up there in front of the room.

When the bell for the afternoon recess rang, Trish put her paper away. If she went outside it might help. She watched Cindy and Sally rush out the door together again. Trish sighed and pulled on her coat.

The bright sunshine made her feel a little better. She saw Sally and Cindy across the playground jumping double with Cindy's jump rope. Trish walked slowly, moving in their direction. She hadn't come out to talk to Sally. She needed some fresh air—that was all. And if Cindy and Sally happened to be jumping rope where she was walking she would just walk right past them. The playground belong to everybody.

Of course it would be nice if Sally stopped jumping rope when she saw her and ran up to her and said, "Please, Trish, let me help you tell about the rats the way we planned. I remember everything we learned. I'll be glad to help you out." It would be nice if Sally did that. But Trish would just smile her nicest smile and say, "No, thank you, Sally. I can do it all by myself."

Of course if Sally begged her really hard, she would have to give in and let Sally help. She would even say, "It's very nice of you to offer. But I could have done it all alone, you know."

Trish didn't turn her head as she passed the two girls. But she watched them out of the corner of her eye. They were having so much fun Trish was sure they didn't notice her at all.

When the bell rang to go back inside, Sally and Cindy ran into the building together. Trish walked back to Mrs. Martin's room alone. Some of the children were crowded around the science table again. Trish went straight to her seat. She didn't want to see the rats. She wished they weren't there at all.

"If you people will take your seats, we will get on with our math test," Mrs. Martin said. "As soon as we are finished, you will hear all about the rats." She took a stack of papers from her desk and handed them to Stanley, who was class monitor for the week. "When you have completed your test, turn your papers over on your desks and sit quietly," Mrs. Martin continued. "Stanley will collect them when the time is up."

Now I won't have time to write anything down about the rats, Trish thought as Stanley passed out the papers and returned to his seat.

Mrs. Martin looked around the room. "Is everyone ready?" A chorus of *yes*'s filled the room. "You have thirty minutes," Mrs. Martin looked at the clock and paused. "You may begin."

The scratch of pencils and an occasional shuffling of feet were the only sounds in the room. Trish worked the first problem, knew it was wrong, erased the answer, and started over again. She glanced at the clock. Only twenty-five minutes left. She had to remember something about the rats. She just had to. Everyone would laugh and make fun of her the way they did in the second grade. She never wanted *that* to happen again. She tried to forget about the rats and concentrate on the math problem again. Maybe if I don't think about it I'll remember something, she thought.

Suddenly Debbie screamed and leaped out of her seat. Mrs. Martin got up from her desk and hurried down the aisle. "Debbie, what's the matter with you? What happened?" she asked.

Debbie pointed with a trembling finger. "There was a mouse on my desk!" Everyone stood up to get a better look.

"Well, it isn't there now," Mrs. Martin said reassuringly. "Perhaps you were mistaken. Now suppose you all get on with your work."

"But I saw it!" Debbie insisted.

"Hey, all of the little rats are out!" Paula shouted.

Trish turned around and looked back at the cage. The top had been pulled partway off. Only Mr. and Mrs. Longtails were still in the cage. "Oh no!" Trish moaned. She looked at Herbie. He was the only one in the whole room still working on his math test. That Herbie! Trish thought, I'll bet he's the one who did that.

"There goes one!" Bruce shouted. Some of the girls screamed and climbed up onto their seats.

"There's one over here," Jimmy yelled from across the room. "I'll get it!"

Trish leaped out of her seat and started toward Jimmy. With everyone milling around she couldn't see any of the rats. "Don't hurt it," she called.

Mrs. Martin rapped loudly on her desk with her ruler. "Return to your seats," she ordered.

Two of the girls started back to their seats; then Paula shouted, "I see one!" She crawled under a desk after it. Barbara screamed and climbed on top of her desk.

"There's one over here," someone shouted. Three boys stampeded toward the back of the room.

"Let me catch it," Trish pleaded as she hurried toward them. No one paid any attention to her. She caught a glimpse of Jumper as the little rat scurried under Robert's desk.

"I got one!" Bruce shouted triumphantly from the back of the room. He held Whiskers up by the tail.

"Don't hurt him!" Trish shouted. She pushed her way through the crowded aisle. "Give him to me!" Bruce was surrounded before she could reach him. Everyone pushed and jostled each other to get a better look.

"There goes another one!" Peter yelled. Bruce turned to look. A hand reached out and grabbed Whiskers. Someone shoved

Whiskers into Trish's hand as the crowd moved like a tidal wave across the room after Peter.

Whisker's heart beat wildly as Trish held him close for a minute. Trish climbed over Herbie's empty seat and put Whiskers back into the cage. She pushed the top down tight and rushed after the crowd. Peter and Herbie were closing in on another rat. Trish started to push her way through the group of boys.

"What is the meaning of this?" Mr. Plunkett's voice boomed above the noise.

Everyone stopped.

Mr. Plunkett Helps

"Has this whole class taken leave of their senses!" Mr. Plunkett roared. He was a tall man with a shiny bald head and a fringe of black hair in the back. He wore dark-rimmed glasses, and his big black mustache always wiggled when he smiled. But now his face looked like a thunder-cloud. "Return to your seats at once!" he shouted. Everyone rushed to obey.

When it was quiet again Mr. Plunkett turned to Mrs. Martin. "Would you mind explaining what this is all about. I could hear your class all the way down to my office." Trish had never seen him look so cross.

Mrs. Martin dabbed her forehead with a handkerchief. "Trish Delaney brought her pet rats to show the class. The little ones seem to have gotten out. The children were trying to catch them."

Mr. Plunkett spun around to face the class. "Patricia Delaney, stand up!" he ordered.

Trish's heart almost leaped out of her chest. What was he going to do with her? Would he march her down to the office and call the police? Did you have to go to jail if you brought rats to school and they got out and made lots of trouble? She had never heard of Mr. Plunkett sending anyone to jail before, but nobody had ever brought rats to school before either. Trish's knees felt all wobbly as she stood up.

"Patricia, you will catch your little pets at once and return them to their cage," Mr. Plunkett said.

Maybe he wasn't going to send her to jail after all! Trish

73

swallowed hard. "Y-yes, sir," she said.

"The rest of you people will remain in your seats. However, if you see one of the rats you may raise your hand and tell Patricia where it is. And do it quietly," he added.

Barbara's hand shot up and waved wildly in the air. "There's one over here!" she shrieked. "It's right by my desk!"

Trish hurried across the room to Barbara's row. Barbara had her feet pulled upon her seat, and her eyes were wide with fright. Trish looked around and found Taffy crouched beside the leg of Barbara's desk. The poor little rat looked as frightened as Barbara.

"Catch it quick before it bites me," Barbara wailed.

Trish almost giggled. How could anyone be afraid of Taffy? She reached down slowly and picked Taffy up, then walked to the back of the room and put her in the cage.

"There. You see how easily this can be done," Mr. Plunkett said. "There is no need at all for a lot of commotion."

Debbie's hand flew up. "I see one over here by the bookcase," she cried. "Hurry quick!" Nosy was no trouble at all to catch. He ran right into Trish's hands. She was glad he was safe. Fredrick would feel awful if anything happened to Nosy. She held him close and carried him back to the cage.

Tommy and Bruce both raised their hands at the same time. "Over here!" Tommy called. Trish started toward him.

"I see one too!" Bruce yelled. Trish stopped and looked from one to the other, not sure which rat to catch first.

Mr. Plunkett walked briskly down the aisle toward Bruce. "You catch that one over there, Patricia. I'll have this little fellow in no time."

By the time Trish reached Tommy's desk, the rat was gone. "It ran under the seat," Tommy said.

Trish slipped through Angela's empty seat into the next aisle. Mr. Plunkett was down on his hands and knees at the front end of the aisle. Trish saw Digger too, but it was too late to warn Mr. Plunkett, Digger leaped and disappeared down the back of Mr. Plunkett's jacket.

"Whoa ho ho!" Mr. Plunkett bellowed. He raised up so suddenly he bumped his head on Julie's desk. He leaped to his feet with one hand on his head and the other behind him. He pranced and wiggled and twisted as though he were doing a new kind of dance.

"Oh my goodness," Mrs. Martin exclaimed. "What's wrong?"

Mr. Plunkett suddenly bent sideways and grabbed his left side. Then he straightened up and put both hands behind him. Everyone roared with laughter, except Trish. She wished she had never taken the rats from Rory Johnson. It wasn't a bit funny—it was terrible. She started to the front of the room. If she could get Mr. Plunkett to stand still long enough, she could catch Digger.

Mr. Plunkett twisted around again with his back to the class. Suddenly Digger jumped out from under his jacket and streaked across Julie's desk. Trish grabbed him before he could get away again.

Mr. Plunkett felt around the back of his jacket, then around the sides and in the front. He straightened up and smoothed his fringe of hair. He adjusted his lopsided glasses as he turned toward the class. His face was red and damp. Suddenly the room became very quiet. Mr. Plunkett cleared his throat. "Patricia, when you have captured the rest of your pets, you will take them home at once. The rest of you people are to remain in your seats. I do not want to hear a single disturbance from this room." He marched out the door and closed it firmly behind him.

No one spoke above a whisper while Trish caught the rest of the rats. She caught Spot on the bottom shelf of the bookcase and put him back in the cage. She closed the top of the cage and made sure it was down tight.

"Is that the last one?" Mrs. Martin asked. Trish nodded. "Then you may be excused," she said.

Trish went back to her desk to put her things away. Now that all of the excitement was over, the class lost interest in the rats.

Stanley raised his hand. "How much time do we have left to finish our math test?" he asked.

"You won't be able to finish it today," Mrs. Martin said. Someone cheered softly from the back of the room. "I'm afraid you will have to take it over again tomorrow. There has been too much confusion to accept the papers you did today." Everyone groaned and looked at Trish.

Trish felt her face grow hot as she picked up the cage. She wanted to tell Mrs. Martin how sorry she was for the way things turned out. But she didn't know what to say. She left the room and hurried down the long, empty hall. She could hardly wait to get home.

Mrs. Peabody opened her door and peeked out into the hall as Trish got out of the elevator. Trish pretended not to see her as she set the cage down and fumbled for the key. She felt around her neck, but she couldn't find the chain. Had she forgotten to put it on this morning? She could feel Mrs. Peabody's eyes on her. Trish wished she would go away. Trish rang the doorbell. Being scolded for forgetting her key was better than standing in the hall being stared at. She rang the doorbell again.

"No use wearing out that bell," Mrs. Peabody called. "Your mother and Fredrick left ten minutes ago." Trish burst into tears.

Mrs. Peabody came down the hall. "Here now, none of that. Come on over to my place until your mother comes back." She led Trish back to her apartment and seated her on the sofa. "Now tell me what this is all about," Mrs. Peabody said in a soft, gentle voice.

Suddenly Trish buried her face in Mrs. Peabody's bony, old shoulder and sobbed out the whole story.

"It was just awful. Mrs. Martin will never like me anymore. And Mr. Plunkett will be mad at me forever. Sally isn't my best friend anymore, and all of the kids are mad at me because they have to take the math test over. I'm never going back to school again. Not ever!"

Mrs. Peabody handed Trish a tissue. "Nothing is ever so bad it can't be mended," she said. "These things happen. It's nothing to get so worked up about." She took Trish by the shoulders and held her at arm's length. "If you had any spunk you'd go right back to the school and get this whole thing straightened out."

Trish jerked her head up and stared at Mrs. Peabody. "I'm never going back to school again. Everybody hates me!"

"Humph!" Mrs. Peabody snorted. "Of course they do. You let

all of the rats out of the cage on purpose. It's all your fault they raised such a ruckus."

"No it wasn't!" Trish cried. "I didn't do anything wrong."

"Then you have nothing to be ashamed of," Mrs. Peabody reminded her. "You're just afraid to speak up and tell folks what's on your mind."

"I am not!" Trish denied quickly.

"Course you are," Mrs. Peabody said. "You have got no more spunk than a marshmallow."

"Yes I do! I could go back to school right this minute and talk to Mrs. Martin and Mr. Plunkett if I wanted to."

"Fiddlesticks!" Mrs. Peabody snorted. "You wouldn't get as far as the corner."

"Yes I will!" Trish got up and scrubbed the tears from her face with the back of her hand. Then she dashed out the door.

Trish ran all the way to school. She jerked open the door and rushed down the hall toward Mrs. Martin's room. Suddenly she noticed how quiet the whole building seemed to be. Everyone had gone home. Trish's knees shook like jelly as she walked slowly down the hall.

Maybe Mrs. Peabody is right, she thought. I don't want to talk to Mrs. Martin and Mr. Plunkett when they're so mad at me. Trish peeked into Mrs. Martin's room. If she isn't here, I'll go home, Trish thought.

"Why, Trish, we were just talking about you." Mrs. Martin looked surprised to see her, and so did Mr. Plunkett.

Trish put her hands behind her and twisted her fingers together as she stepped into the room. "I came to say I'm sorry for what happened today." Trish blurted out the words in a rush. There, she'd said it!

"Mrs. Martin assures me that what happened today was an accident," Mr. Plunkett said. He leaned forward and shook his finger at Trish. "Of course if this had been a prank, it would be a different matter."

"Oh, it wasn't!" Trish said quickly. "I never meant for the rats to get out and cause so much trouble. And I'm sorry for what Digger did to you. He didn't mean it. He was just scared and wanted a place to hide."

Mr. Plunkett's mustache wiggled when he smiled. "Well, I suppose we can forgive Digger for that," he said. Trish began to feel much better.

"Trish has always been one of my most cooperative students," Mrs. Martin said. "I'm sure she would never do anything to deliberately disrupt the class."

"Oh no," Trish assured them. "I don't know how the top of the cage came lose. I think it was Her—" Trish stopped. It wouldn't be fair to blame Herbie. After all, she hadn't really seen him open the cage. "I should have made sure the top was on tight after recess," she said.

"I appreciate your coming back to get this straightened out," Mr. Plunkett said. "Run along home now, and the next time you bring a pet to school, be sure the cage is properly fastened."

"I'll see you tomorrow, Trish," Mrs. Martin said. "Perhaps some other time you can bring the rats again and tell the class about them."

Trish hoped Mrs. Martin would never, ever mention bringing the rats to school again. "Goodbye," Trish said. "See you tomorrow."

Trish skipped all the way home. She felt wonderful. She could hardly wait to tell Mrs. Peabody all about it. I wasn't scared at all, she thought. Not very much anyway.

Mother met Trish as she stepped out of the elevator. "There you are. I've been worried about you," she said.

"I had to go back to school for something," Trish explained. She started down the hall. "I want to tell Mrs. Peabody something. I'll be right back."

"Whatever it is will have to wait," Mom said. "I must talk to you right away. It's very important."

No Place for Rats

Trish followed her mother into the dining room. "I came straight home from school, but I had to go back again," she explained.

"You can tell me about it later," her mother said. "Right now I want to talk to you about Lynne. Sit down, Trish."

"What's Lynne complaining about now?" Trish asked. "Did I do something wrong?" Trish frowned and slumped into her chair.

Her mother sat down across the table and reached for Trish's hand. "We got the report back from Dr. Wright today on Lynne's tests." The little frown lines came out on Mother's forehead.

"Is Lynne very sick?" Trish wished now she had been nicer to Lynne.

Mother smiled and squeezed Trish's hand. "It's not that bad, but I need your help so Lynne can get well."

"Me?" Trish gasped. "How can I help?"

"By giving away your rats," Mother said.

Trish pulled her hand away. "That' not fair! Just because Lynne doesn't like them and she's sick—"

"You don't understand, Trish," Mom interrupted. "Lynne's dislike for the rats has nothing to do with it. The tests show that Lynne is allergic to animal hair. Rat hair to be exact. They are the only animals Lynne has come in contact with, so I took some samples of their hair to Dr. Wright, and he ran another test."

"But Lynne didn't even touch them," Trish protested. "How could they make her sick?"

"Lynne doesn't have to touch them," her mother explained. "Just being in the same apartment with them is enough. She will always have watery eyes and sneeze as long as the rats are here."

"Oh," Trish mumbled. She got up from the table and started to leave the room.

"Wait, Trish." Her mother stood up and put her arm around Trish. "I know how much the rats mean to you, Honey. I hate to ask you to give them up, but I'm afraid there is nothing else we can do. You do understand, don't you?" She put a finger under Trish's chin and tilted her face up.

Trish nodded. "I guess Lynne would do the same for me if I was sick. When do I have to give them away?"

Mother hugged Trish close. "I know this is going to be hard for you. I've made arrangements for Lynne to stay with Deb for a couple of days to give you time to find a new home for the rats. But I want you to do it as soon as possible."

"I will," Trish promised. She went to her room and looked down at her shelf before she remembered that she hadn't brought the rats in earlier. She hurried back to the dining room. "Mom, did you bring the rats in out of the hall?" she asked.

"Why no," her mother said. "There was nothing in the hall when Fredrick and I came home. He wouldn't be watching cartoons if he'd had a chance to play with Nosy. Why didn't you bring them in yourself?"

"I forgot my key," Trish admitted. "The rats were still in the hall when I went back to school. Maybe somebody stole them."

Mom smiled. "I doubt that."

"Mrs. Peabody must have taken them. I'm going to go see." Trish started for the door.

"Now why would Mrs. Peabody take them?" Mom asked.

"Is it all right if I explain after I bring the rats home?" Trish asked. "I can bring them home, can't I?"

"Yes, of course," her mother said. "Lynne won't be home tonight."

Trish hurried down the hall to Mrs. Peabody's and rang the doorbell. The door flew open almost before Trish took her finger off the bell.

"Well don't just stand there," Mrs. Peabody said. "Come in." She led the way into the living room. "Don't suppose you got to the corner."

Some of the excitement Trish had felt earlier came rushing back. She grinned at Mrs. Peabody. "Yes I did. I talked to Mrs. Martin and Mr. Plunkett, and they're not mad at me anymore."

"Mrs. Peabody's dark eyes twinkled. "I figured you had enough spunk to straighten things out. Now sit down there on the sofa for a minute. I've got a batch of cookies in the oven that need tending to."

Trish perched on the edge of the sofa and looked around. The ticking of the funny-looking old clock on the bookcase sounded loud in the quiet room. Trish hadn't noticed it earlier. The furniture looked as if it came from the museum the family had visited the summer before. Trish had always thought Mrs. Peabody's apartment would be scary, but it wasn't, not even a little bit.

"You take these home for your family's dinner," Mrs. Peabody said as she set a plastic-wrapped plate of cookies on the coffee table.

"They smell good," said Trish. "Peanut-butter cookies are my very favorite. Thank you very much."

Mrs. Peabody smiled with pleasure. "There's nothing like a good chewy cookie fresh from the oven. But there's no sense making a batch all for myself." She settled herself in a rocking chair and looked at Trish. "Now tell me what happened."

Trish told her about the visit to the school and how she happened to take the rats there in the first place. "I almost forgot why I came," she said. "I left my rats out in the hall when I went back to school. Now they're gone. Do you know what happened to them?"

Mrs. Peabody pointed to the far corner of the room with her cane. "I brought them in for safekeeping. Can't have somebody stealing your pets."

Trish sighed. "It wouldn't matter now. I have to give them

away. Lynne is allergic to them. I wish I had never taken them from Rory."

Mrs. Peabody chuckled. "Got yourself in a mess, did you? I had a bunch of fish for a while. I know how it is with pets." She pointed to the huge aquarium against the wall. "My son bought me that contraption and had it filled with fish before he moved to California. Had the foolish notion they would keep me company. Humph! Never cared much for the pesky things."

"Did you have to give them away too?" Trish asked. She looked at the gnarled piece of wood leaning against the glass on the inside of the empty tank and wondered whether it had been there with the fish.

"Course not," Mrs. Peabody said. "I kept them. They weren't much company though. I couldn't talk to them or pet them. Just sat here and watched them swim around. When the last one died a few months ago I never bothered to get any more."

The funny old clock struck the quarter hour. "It's almost time for Dad to come home," Trish said. "I'd better go now." She picked up the cage and started for the door. "Thank you for making the cookies, and thank you for taking care of my rats."

"I'd like to know what you're planning to do with all those things," Mrs. Peabody said. She set the plate on top of the cage and opened the door.

Trish shrugged. "I don't know yet." Mrs. Peabody closed the door. Trish smiled as she started to her own apartment. She didn't know about the rats, but she knew something else. Mrs. Peabody wasn't mean; she was only pretending. She was a nice old lady—and she was lonely.

Trish had time to put the rats in her room and wash her hands before dinner.

"I didn't get to play with my Nosy today," Fredrick complained as he followed Trish to the table.

"You can play with him after dinner," Trish promised.

After Dad asked a blessing on the food, Mom told him all about Lynne's allergy and why Lynne wasn't home.

Dad turned to Trish and said, "I'm afraid this is no place for rats. It's too bad. You've done a good job of taking care of them. Do you know anyone who will take them?"

Trish shook her head. "I'm going to ask the kids at school tomorrow. I'll find a good home for all of them."

"That could take a long time," Dad said. "And you have only two days. Remember, this is Lynne's home too. All the rats have to go."

Fredrick stopped eating. "My Nosy can't go. He has to stay home."

"Nosy—" Trish began. Mom frowned and shook her head. Trish knew that meant, Don't say anything. "Nosy is waiting for you, so finish your dinner," Trish said. Fredrick grinned and dug into his mashed potatoes.

Trish let Fredrick play with the little rat until it was time for bed. "You can play with Nosy in the morning, if it's all right with Mom," she said.

It was strangely quiet in the room after Fredrick went to bed. Trish glanced over at Lynne's bed. I always wondered what it would be like to have a room all my own, she thought. Now I know. It's lonesome.

Trish knelt beside her bed to say her prayers. "Please God," she prayed. "I know I shouldn't ask for things I can do myself. But I can't think of a way for Fredrick to keep Nosy and have Lynne get well too. I want Lynne to come home. I really miss her. And if I give Nosy away, Fredrick will miss him too. Please help me find a way to make them both happy."

The next day at school Trish decided to ask everyone in her class if they wanted a rat, except Sally and Barbara.

"I wish I could have one," said Paula. "I told my mom about them last night, but she won't let me have one."

Herbie came up behind Trish and yanked on her skirt. "I hear you're giving away your rats. I'll take one."

Trish smiled. For the first time she almost liked Herbie. "Which one do you want?"

Herbie grinned. "I'll take the one that ran down Mr. Plunkett's back."

"You can come over and get him right after school if it's all right with you mother," Trish said. "Bring a cage to put him in."

"Aw, I'm not going to keep him in a cage. I'm going to keep

him in my pocket," said Herbie.

"But he can't live in your pocket!" Trish protested. "Digger would suffocate or get smashed."

Herbie shrugged. "So what? He's only a rat."

"Then you can't have him!" Trish cried. She turned her back on Herbie and went to find Stanley.

"I'd like to take them," Stanley said, "But I don't have room for them right now. I'm studying turtles."

Trish spent all of her recesses and most of her lunch hour trying to find someone who would take the rats, but nobody wanted even one. On the way home Trish suddenly had an idea.

"I'm home!" Trish called as she rushed in the door. "May I go to the store?"

"Have you given the rats away?" her mother asked.

"No, but I think I know someone who will take all of them. May I go?"

"All right," Mother said. "I hope you find someone soon."

Trish ran all the way to the store. She went straight to the pet section to see Miss Forrest.

"Hi, Trish," Miss Forrest called. "Did you come to buy a bigger cage?"

Trish shook her head. "I have to give my rats away. My sister is allergic to them. Do you think your aunt would like to have them?"

"Oh, I'm afraid not," Miss Forrest said. "You see my aunt lives several hundred miles away across the state. Why don't you try the pet shop? They might take them."

"The pet shop?" Trish said.

"The one over on Conners," Miss Forrest said. "The owner, Mr. Barkley, might be interested."

"Thank you," Trish said. She walked outside slowly. I wish Lynne was here, she thought. I don't want to go that far all by myself. And what if Mr. Barkley doesn't want the rats? Her knees felt all trembly at the thought of talking to him. She stood there for a long time. It would be easier to go home. But what would she do with the rats? She turned toward home. "I'll do it tomorrow," she told herself.

"You have got no more spunk than a marshmallow," she

could almost hear Mrs. Peabody saying. Trish stopped and looked back down the street. Six blocks wasn't really so far. She took a deep breath and turned around.

A bell tinkled as she opened the pet shop door. A man with gray hair and a friendly face stopped talking to a woman beside the counter and turned to Trish. "Can I help you?" he asked.

Trish's heart thumped against her ribs as she walked toward the counter. "Would—would you like to have some rats?" she asked.

Mr. Barkley pushed his glasses up on his forehead. "How many have you got?"

"Ten," Trish answered. "Eight little ones and two big ones." She began to feel a little bit hopeful. "The baby ones are three weeks old."

"Hum, that's about the right age." Mr. Barkley stroked his chin. "I've had some requests for rats lately. Bring them around tomorrow, and I'll take a look at them."

Trish wanted to leap in the air and shout. "I'll bring them right after school tomorrow," she said and rushed out the door.

It wasn't so hard after all, she thought as she hurried home. Just wait until Mom heard the news.

"You can't give my Nosy away!" Fredrick howled when Trish told her mother about Mr. Barkley.

"If you keep Nosy, Lynne can't come home," Mother explained. "You don't want that to happen do you?"

"Yes!" Fredrick howled louder. "I want my Nosy!"

"Mr. Barkley didn't say he would take them," Trish said. "He's just going to look at them."

"He can't look at my Nosy," Fredrick wailed and rushed off to Trish's room to be with his pet.

Trish Speaks Up

Trish was alone on the playground at school the next day when Lynne called to her. Surprised, Trish turned around. Lynne never spoke to her at school unless it was important. She was always too busy playing with her own friends.

"Have you still got the rats?" Lynne asked. "Mom said you were supposed to give them away today. I'll bet nobody at school has been dumb enough to take them."

Trish shook her head. "Nobody has. But I think Mr. Barkley at the pet shop will take them. I wish I didn't have to give Nosy away. Fredrick really loves him."

"I wish so too," said Lynne. "But I want to come home. I miss you."

"I'm sorry the rats made you sick," said Trish. "If I had known, I never would have taken them from Rory."

"And I'm sorry you have to give them away," said Lynne. "I was getting kinda used to having them around. The little ones are sorta cute." Lynne kicked a pebble off of the walk and shifted from one foot to the other. "You want to go to the science center with me and Deb on Sunday? We're going to the aquarium afterward to see the new dolphins do tricks."

Trish stared at her sister. "Are you sure Deb won't mind if I come?"

Lynne shrugged. "If she does, we'll go without her." She grinned. "See ya later," she said and rushed off as the bell started to ring.

Trish felt almost grown up as she hurried back to Mrs.

Martin's room. Lynne had never asked her to go along to anything before. Lynne took her only when Mom said she had to. When Lynne acted this nice, she almost didn't mind giving away the rats. It would be easy if it wasn't for Nosy and Fredrick. Trish spent the rest of the afternoon trying to think of some way to keep the little rat. But by the time school let out she hadn't thought of any way at all. Fredrick would just have to give him up.

Trish hurried home and went straight to her room to get the rats. She was glad Fredrick was busy watching cartoons.

"Are you sure you can manage that heavy cage all by yourself?" Mother asked. "I wish you could take the bus. I would come along, but I don't want Fredrick getting upset."

"I know," Trish agreed. She picked up the cage. "I'll be quiet, and maybe he won't hear me."

Fredrick looked up as Trish tiptoed past the living room. He was still howling for Nosy when she went out the door. She thought about Nosy and Fredrick as she pushed the elevator button. If only there was some way. Suddenly Trish grinned. "Maybe there is." She hurried down the hall and rang Mrs. Peabody's doorbell.

"Well, don't just stand there. Speak up!" Mrs. Peabody snapped when she opened the door. But her eyes were twinkling.

"I came to ask you something," Trish said as she followed Mrs. Peabody into the living room. She set the cage down on the floor.

Mrs. Peabody eased herself down into her rocking chair and rested her cane against the arm. "Well, get on with it."

Trish explained about Fredrick and Nosy. "Would you let me keep him in your big fish tank? I would come over and feed him every day and clean the cage. He wouldn't be any trouble."

"Humph!" Mrs. Peabody sniffed. "What makes you think I want that rat here?"

Trish grinned. "Because you could talk to him and pet him, and he's fun to watch. Especially when he eats. And sometimes, if you didn't mind, Fredrick could come over to play with him."

Mrs. Peabody chuckled. "Learning to speak up, are you? You

think Nosy would like living here?" Trish nodded. "That tank is too big for one little rat. He'd get lonesome in there all by himself."

"But—" Trish began.

Mrs. Peabody leaned forward and pointed at the cage. "Let me see that little fellow right there. That's the one," she said when Trish reached for Whiskers. "Give him here."

"Be careful," Trish warned. "He might bite; he's not used to you."

"Oh bosh," Mrs. Peabody exclaimed. "He didn't bite the other day. Now get that Nosy out of there and put him in the aquarium with this one."

Nosy and Whiskers scampered up and over the gnarled piece of wood, then scurried around the bottom of the aquarium, examining every inch of space.

"I guess those two will do," Mrs. Peabody said. "Looks like they're satisfied with their new home."

"You mean you'll keep them?" Trish cried.

The old-fashioned clock struck four. Trish gasped. "I told Mr. Barkley I'd bring the rats right after school. I'll be back later with food and shavings for the bottom of the cage. Thanks, Mrs. Peabody." She grabbed up the cage and hurried out the door.

An hour later Trish burst into her own apartment. "The rats are gone!" she cried. "Lynne can come home." She dropped her packages into a chair.

Fredrick's eyes were still red and puffy from crying. He hiccuped, and his face puckered up again when he saw Trish. "I want my Nosy," he wailed. "I want my Nosy."

Trish knelt beside him and put her arms around him. "I couldn't bring Nosy home," she said. "But you can see him whenever you want."

Mother rubbed her fingers across her forehead and sighed. "Please, Trish. Don't tell him that. He's going to make himself sick if he doesn't stop crying over that rat."

Trish stood up. "But he can see Nosy. Mrs. Peabody is keeping him for us. Fredrick can come over there with me right now. I promised to bring the food and shavings over as soon as I got back. Mr. Barkley, at the pet shop traded me a big bag of shavings, a box of food, and an exercise wheel for the rest of the rats."

Fredrick yanked on Trish's hand. "I want to go see my Nosy right now!" He laughed and jumped up and down.

Mother threw her hands in the air. "For goodness sakes, Trish, take him to see Nosy. Later you can tell me everything that happened. While you're gone I'll call Lynne and tell her she can come home. It will be nice to have things back to normal again."

Trish said a silent prayer of thanks and took Fredrick down the hall to Mrs. Peabody's.

Rats and Roller Skates

The next day at school Trish stood alone on the playground deep in thought. Mom had said things would be back to normal again, and that was partly true. Lynne was home again, and she wasn't sneezing anymore. Fredrick was able to go over to Mrs. Peabody's to see Nosy anytime he wanted to. But Sally wasn't her best friend anymore.

Trish looked around the playground. Cindy and Angela were jumping rope near the monkey bars. But Sally was not with them. Now that Angela was back, Angela and Cindy were best friends again. Trish finally saw Sally sitting alone on the steps. Trish walked slowly around the playground where Sally would be sure to see her.

Maybe Sally will speak to me now that she is alone too, Trish thought. She came closer to Sally and stopped. She could see that Sally was wearing the new blue dress that her grandmother had made for her. Trish wanted to tell Sally how pretty it was. But she thought Sally should speak first. The longer Trish waited, the angrier she got. Why did Sally have to be so stubborn? They were never going to be best friends again if she didn't say something soon.

Finally Sally stood up. Trish's heart began to beat faster. Now Sally would come over and talk to her! But Sally turned and went into the building. Trish walked over and leaned against the brick wall. She would *not* follow Sally inside! She would stay out here and wait for the bell to ring. She had given Sally every chance to say she was sorry. Now she knew Sally didn't want to be friends with her again.

The day dragged by even more slowly than Fridays. Trish wished it would hurry and be over so she could go home. Several times she looked across the aisle at Sally. Once they looked at each other at the same time and quickly looked away again. Trish felt tears sting her eyes as she bent over her spelling.

When science period came, Trish took out her book with a feeling of relief. It was the last lesson of the day. She could go home soon.

"Maybe we'll be studying about rats today," Herbie said in a loud whisper. Some of the other boys snickered and made noises like a rat.

Mrs. Martin snapped her book shut. "There has been a lot of discussion about rats in this class the last couple of days. Since you people have shown such an interest in the subject, I am going to ask Trish to tell us about them. Trish, will you come up here please."

Trish suddenly felt cold all over. She could never get up in front of the whole class alone! Everybody turned to look at her. Trish's knees trembled as she slid out of her seat. She walked slowly to the front of the room. If she only had her book or the notes she had made. Or best of all, if Sally could be there beside her. She turned to face the class and thought for a moment that she was going to be sick. She couldn't remember one single thing about the rats.

"You may begin, Trish." Mrs. Martin smiled at her.

Trish felt her face grow hot. She put her hands behind her back and twisted her fingers together. She tried to look at the sea of faces, but that didn't help. If I can only remember something, she thought desperately. Even the rats' names.

Trish took a deep breath. "Rats have long tails," she blurted out in a high, squeaky voice. Everyone laughed.

Trish wanted to run and hide, but she couldn't move. She could feel the tears filling up behind her eyes. The faces in front of her were getting all blurry. Trish blinked quickly. It would be awful if she cried right there in front of everybody.

"Where's your spunk?" Mrs. Peabody's gruff old voice seemed to be saying in her ear. "Don't just stand there. Speak up!"

Trish swallowed hard. "Rats use their tails for balance." This time her voice sounded more like her own.

Slowly the blur of faces separated and turned into Paula and Joe and Barbara and Stanley. They were her friends. She talked to them every day. Why should standing up here in front of all of them at once be so different? Maybe some of them felt the same way when they had to stand up here. Suddenly everything she had learned about the rats came crowding back into her mind. The class looked at her expectantly as they waited for her to continue.

Several hands went up when Trish finished. She was still answering questions when Mrs. Martin interrupted.

"Time is up," she said. "Put your things away before the bell rings."

Trish glowed with satisfaction as she walked back to her seat. It hadn't been as hard as she thought. Now she had one more thing to do.

Trish was waiting when Sally came out of the building. Trish marched right up to her and said, "I have something to tell you. The skates you saw in my closet belong to my sister, Lynne. I never went roller-skating with you because I don't know how, and I've been afraid to learn. I wish we could be friends again."

"I'm sorry Muffin tried to catch Taffy," Sally said, looking down at her shoes. "I never thought he would want to eat a rat."

"It was my fault too," Trish admitted, trying to take her share of the blame. "I knew you had a cat. I should have remembered cats like to eat rats too."

Sally drew an imaginary line on the sidewalk with her toe. "I was the one who took Whiskers away from Bruce. And I wanted to help you tell about the rats today like we planned. But I thought you were still mad at me."

Trish gasped. "You did? I thought you were still mad at me, or I would have asked you." As they started home she told Sally all about everything that had happened since she brought the rats to school. "Can you come over today? We can go to Mrs. Peabody's and see two of the baby rats. She's keeping Nosy and Whiskers."

"I have to go home and change my dress first," Sally said.

"Mom won't let me use my skates or play or anything when I'm wearing it. She says Grandma worked hard making it, and I have to take care of it."

"I think it's a very pretty dress," Trish said. "I wish my Mom could sew like that."

They stopped at the crosswalk. Mr. Bailey motioned for them to cross and smiled at them as they passed.

"Don't take too long," Trish said when they reached the other side.

"I won't. I'll skate over to your building," Sally called and rushed down the street.

Trish ran all the way home. She had something very important to do before Sally came.

Trish was waiting in the hall when Sally got off the elevator.

Sally looked at Trish and gasped. "But I thought—" she began.

Trish smiled. "Mom let me buy them. I decided I'm not going to be a sissy about skating anymore. Will you help me learn how after we see the rats?"·

Sally nodded. "I smell something good," she said.

"Mrs. Peabody must be baking cookies again," said Trish. "Let's go see."

Sally took Trish's arm, and Trish wobbled down the hall on her new roller skates. They grinned at each other as Trish rang Mrs. Peabody's doorbell. It was wonderful to be best friends again.